From Concept to Screen

From Concept to Screen

An Overview of Film and Television Production

Robert Benedetti

Allyn and Bacon

Boston • London • Toronto • Sydney • Tokyo • Singapore

Series Editor: *Molly Taylor*
Editorial-Production Service: *Nesbitt Graphics, Inc.*

Library of Congress Cataloging-in-Publication Data

Benedetti, Robert L.
    From concept to screen : an overview of film and television production /
by Robert Benedetti.
        p. cm.
    Includes bibliographical references and index.
    ISBN 0-205-32743-5 (alk. paper)
    1. Motion pictures—Production and direction.   I. Title.

PN1995.9.P7 B36 2001
791.43'0232—dc21

                                                                    2001018165

Printed in the United States of America

10 9 8 7 6 5 4 3 2   06 05 04

This book is dedicated to Joe Sargent,
a great director and even greater human being.

CONTENTS

FIGURES

PREFACE

Those who know my books on acting (*The Actor at Work*, *The Actor in You*, and *ACTION! Acting for Film and Television*) may be surprised to find me writing a book on film and television production. Ten years ago, after teaching acting for almost 30 years, I decided I needed a new challenge. One of my actor friends suggested that with my various creative and administrative skills, I would make a good producer. Luckily, another friend and ex-student, Ted Danson, had a production company at Paramount, and he agreed to let me "hang around" and learn the business. I took a sabbatical, and one thing led to another; a year later I was running the company.

Four years later, *Cheers* ended and Ted's company ended with it, but I was by then established and formed my own company. I have been an independent producer ever since and have had the good fortune to work with passionate artists for intelligent companies on worthwhile projects.

Throughout this book I will give examples from one such film, HBO's *Miss Evers' Boys*, which starred Alfre Woodard and Laurence Fishburne. It was written by Walter Bernstein from a play by David Feldshuh and directed by Joseph Sargent. It is available as a video rental, and viewing it early on will enhance your understanding of my examples.

ACKNOWLEDGMENTS

The manuscript for this book was reviewed by several working professionals who made extremely helpful comments and corrections. Those deserving special thanks are:

Derek Kavanagh, producer and UPM of many films, including five of the *Pink Panther* films, *Dances with Wolves*, and *Miss Evers' Boys*. He was formerly Vice President of Production for United Artists.

Vance Van Petten, Executive Director of the Producers Guild of America. He was formerly Head of Legal Affairs at Studio USA and Universal Television, and formerly with 20th Century Fox Television Business Affairs.

Bernie Laramie, formerly Director of Post Production at Lorimar and consultant to Lucasfilm's Droidworks. He has pioneered many state-of-the-art techniques for electronic editing and special effects and is currently co-producer of *C.S.I.* on CBS.

Benjamin Benedetti, former Head of Postproduction for *The Disney Channel*, now with Digital Symphony.

Michael Schwartz, sales coordinator for the Sony High Definition Center, and Terry Brown, Chief Engineer of the Laserpacific Media Corporation, for their help researching the chapter on High Definition Digital Television.

Thanks also to the academic reviewers: Ken Dancyger, New York University; Ian Maitland, New York University; Kristine Samuelson, Stanford University; and James B. Steerman, Vassar College. And thanks to my editor, Karon Bowers, and the other fine people at Allyn & Bacon.

ABOUT THE AUTHOR

For the past 12 years, Robert Benedetti has been a film and television writer-producer and recently won Emmy and Humanitas awards for the HBO films, *Miss Evers' Boys* and *A Lesson Before Dying*, the latter also winning a Peabody Award. Benedetti also produced the Showtime film, *Aldrich Ames: Traitor Within*, which was nominated for a WGA Award. He also wrote and produced *Mercy Mission* for NBC, and *The Canterville Ghost* for ABC, which was named Best Family Film of 1996. In 1995 he produced *On Promised Land* for the Disney Channel, which won the CableAce Award. He was Executive Producer of the Paramount feature film, *Pontiac Moon*. In 1997 he was named Producer of the Year by the Producers Guild of America. Before beginning his producing career, Benedetti was Dean of the School of Theater at the California Institute of the Arts and Chairman of the Acting Program at the Yale Drama School. He has directed at numerous theaters and festivals, including the Tyrone Guthrie Theater, the Oregon Shakespearean Festival, the Melbourne Theater Company, and many others. His book, *The Actor at Work,* has been a best-selling acting text for 30 years and is now in its eighth edition. He also wrote *The Director at Work* and recently published *The Actor in You* and *ACTION! Acting for Film and Television.* Benedetti holds a Ph.D. from Northwestern University.

1   The Producer

This book describes how a film is created, from conception to screen, and is intended to enhance the understanding and appreciation of anyone interested in film in all its various forms. It presents an overview of the production process and its relationship to the artistic aspects of filmmaking. It is not intended as a "how to" book, so only a limited amount of technical detail is included.

I will focus on four kinds of films: theatrical films (**features**) made by major studios; independently financed feature films (**indies**); movies made for network television (often called **MOW**s for "Movie of the Week"); and movies *made-for-cable* television. These films are all *narrative long-form*, which means that they tell a story and are more than 1 hour long. I will also discuss 1-hour episodic network television shows (such as *ER* and *Law and Order*) and half-hour, multiple-camera television shows (sitcoms and soap operas). Although there are differences in the way each of these kinds of films are made, I will focus on the underlying principles and processes that are common to all of them. Along the way, I will explain many terms that are used in film and television production. These are printed in **bold** when they first appear, and they are listed in the *Glossary* at the end of the book, along with many other film terms.

The Producer

The person who is most responsible for guiding the filmmaking process from start to finish is the **producer** (in television, often called the **executive producer**). The producer is the central intelligence of a film project. He or she conceives or selects the basic idea for the film, then sells it to a studio or network or arranges independent financing. He or she then selects the writer and guides the writing of the script, selects the director, works with the director and the network or studio to cast the show and select the key creative team, supervises the production process, then oversees the post-production process leading to final delivery. After completion, the producer may also be involved in marketing and distribution.

In each phase of this long and complex process, the producer is responsible for keeping the project true to its creative essence, while at the same time making the many compromises necessary to best utilize the available resources of time, money, and personnel. In this sense, the producer is *the traffic cop at the intersection of art and commerce.*

The day-to-day responsibilities of the producer vary in different situations. They have never been specified by a union or guild in the way that the Directors Guild of America (**DGA**), Writers Guild of America (**WGA**), or Screen Actors Guild (**SAG**) have defined and negotiated the responsibilities and rights of their members, so there is some confusion about what a producer does, or even who should receive credit as a producer. To make matters worse, there has been an alarming proliferation of producer credits in this decade, with credits such as co-executive producer, co-producer, and associate producer given to writers, directors, actors, financiers, and many others who may or may not actually serve a producing function.

In 1999, the Producers Guild of America (**PGA**) developed a complete list of the functions of a producer in an effort to standardize the responsibilities of a producer and to define legitimate producing credits. Besides its intended functions, the PGA list also provides a comprehensive description of the producer's work and a chronological view of the major creative and commercial decisions that are involved in the process of filmmaking itself. Though some of the terms and processes to which the list refers may be unclear to you now, they will all be explained in the chapters that follow. I recommend that you review this list at various times as your understanding of the filmmaking process grows.

PGA Motion Picture Producing Functions

Development/Pre-Production

1. Conceiving the underlying concept on which the production is based.
2. Selecting the material on which the production is based.
3. Securing necessary rights for development and production of the material.
4. Selecting the screenwriter.
5. Supervising and overseeing the development process (i.e., the overall process of how the concept is developed into the screenplay/teleplay).
6. Securing the initial financing (e.g., studio or independent funding, license fees, loans).
7. Serving as the primary point of contact for the network or studio.
8. Selecting the unit production manager.

9. Preparing the preliminary budget.
10. Selecting the director.
11. Selecting the principal cast.
12. Selecting the production designer.
13. Selecting the cinematographer.
14. Selecting the editor.
15. Approving the final shooting schedule.
16. Approving and signing the final budget.
17. Approving and signing the final shooting script.

Production

18. Overseeing and approving the deals for the principal components of the production.
19. Supervising the unit production manager.
20. Providing in-person consultation with the director.
21. Providing in-person consultation with the principal cast.
22. Providing in-person consultation with the production designer.
23. Providing in-person consultation with the cinematographer.
24. Selecting the composer.
25. Providing in-person consultation on the set design, set dressings, locations, and props.
26. Providing in-person consultation on visual and mechanical effects, if any.
27. Providing in-person consultation on wardrobe, makeup, and hair.
28. Managing and approving the weekly cost report.
29. Supervising the day-to-day operation of the shooting company and of all talent and crafts.
30. Supervising in person the operations of the shoot, talent, and crafts when on location.
31. Viewing the dailies and providing in-person consultation with the director and the editor.

Post-Production

32. Providing in-person consultation with the editor.
33. Providing in-person consultation with the composer.
34. Viewing and appraising the director's cut.
35. Participating in-person in the attainment and approval of the final cut.
36. Supervising the music recording sessions.
37. Supervising the re-recording sessions.
38. Supervising the titles and opticals.
39. Participating in-person in the preview process.
40. Providing in-person consultation on the answer print or edited master.

41. Providing in-person consultation on the marketing plan and materials.
42. Providing in-person consultation on the plan of distribution/exploitation.
43. Participating in-person in the publicity process.
44. Participating in-person in the exploitation in ancillary markets.[1]

The PGA made this list as complete as possible, understanding that not all producers in all situations will necessarily be required to do everything it includes. For instance, producers of television movies are rarely involved in the marketing efforts of the network or cable company. Conversely, though the list is a complete description of a typical filmmaking process, it does not cover many unique situations that may arise in the course of any particular film project. Producing is, more than anything else, *problem-solving*. A good producer thinks well on his or her feet, and not only solves but tries to anticipate and prevent problems.

Though the PGA list implies that the producer makes all these crucial decisions, in actual practice the producer's authority is always shared with, and subservient to, that of the financing entity—the film studio, the TV network, the cable outlet, or the group of independent investors. Although the producer defines and suggests choices and, once approved, executes them, the financing entity will have ultimate approval over the producer's decisions. The only exceptions to this rule are those rare and wonderful situations in which the producer also controls the financing, or where the producer has won creative control. This is increasingly rare today, but in the golden days of the studio system, it was the norm. Just a few decades ago, studios were slow to intrude on a producer's creative control. Albert J. Broccoli and Blake Edwards, for example, had total control over the *James Bond* and *Pink Panther* movies. Today, only a few powerful producers have a significant amount of control: in feature film, this includes producers such as Jerry Bruckheimer (*Flashdance*, the *Beverly Hills Cop* series, *Pearl Harbor*), and Joel Silver (the *Lethal Weapon* series, *The Matrix*); in television, successful series producers such as Steven Bochco (*Hill Street Blues*, *LA Law*, *NYPD Blue*), David E. Kelley (*The Practice*, *Ally McBeal*), and John Wells (*ER*, *The West Wing*, *Third Watch*.)

Producing is a risky business. Producers do not usually receive any income from a project until filming actually begins. If a project is abandoned before production begins, the producer makes nothing—and may actually lose money. Until the first money comes in, then, a producer needs to find a source of operating funds. Successful producers may procure such funds by forming a liaison with a studio or production company. The simplest of these is a **first-look** deal in which a producer gives a company the first opportunity to participate in any project he or she initiates; in return, the producer may receive **housekeeping** support in the form of office space and access to basic services. More generous first-look deals may include a guaranteed minimum annual fee as an **advance** against future projects.

Although producer deals have become increasingly rare in the industry, major stars often receive them for the purpose of encouraging their loyalty to a particular studio. I was fortunate to get my start as a producer running such a company for Ted Danson at Paramount Pictures. Ted and I were committed to making movies that would encourage audiences to adopt a more caring and responsible attitude toward other people and the planet, and this has remained my motivation as a producer ever since. For this reason, I have worked mainly in the arena of cable television, for companies like HBO and Showtime, where it is possible to do quality work driven by a sense of social purpose. As we move fully into the information age and the media become omnipresent in our lives, it will be increasingly important for producers and industry executives to exercise ethical responsibility, despite the bottom line pressure from the remote and anonymous multinational corporations that have come to control the film and television industries.

Choosing an Underlying Concept

As the PGA list indicates, the first function of the producer is to conceive "the underlying concept on which the production will be based." Some concepts lend themselves to film more readily than do others, and the producer must have a sense of what constitutes a good cinematic story.

When judging a potential story, the producer should remember that film is more a *visual* than a *verbal* medium. Although it is widely agreed that a good film starts with a good script, the script for a film differs from a novel or stage play in that its orientation is mainly visual. Although the dialogue should specify and enrich the story, the fundamental action of the story is best expressed through images. Moreover, a film consists of a fixed *sequence* of images. This sequence itself can produce meanings and emotional richness that transcend the meaning of the individual images. The great director Sergei Eisenstein put it this way:

> Two pieces of [film], placed together, inevitably combine into a new concept, a new quality, arising out of that juxtaposition . . . For example, take a grave, juxtaposed with a woman in mourning weeping beside it, and scarcely anybody will fail to jump to the conclusion: **a widow**.[2]

Eisenstein called this power of sequential images to produce new meanings the **montage** effect. This effect applied not only to specific images, as in the example, but to the overall construction of the film as well. As he said:

> [There is in film] the need for connected and sequential exposition of the theme, the material, the plot, the action, the movement within the film sequence and within the film drama as a whole. . . . Our films [must present] not only a

narrative that is logically connected, but one that contains a maximum of emotion and stimulating power.[3]

To best serve as the basis for a film, a story must *be capable of being told through a sequence of connected images that lead with unbroken momentum toward the climax.* Perhaps the greatest example of this is Orson Welles' *Citizen Kane* in which the evolving mystery of the protagonist's life climaxes in a final revelatory image of "Rosebud," a boyhood sled, burning.

The need for a cinematic story to have momentum and flow toward a climax discourages the producer from pursuing stories that are too strongly episodic, as well as stories that depend on rapid shifts between multiple points of view. Although such stories may make successful films in the hands of a director with a particular vision (for example, John Huston's interpretation of James Joyce's *The Dead*), they are extremely difficult to translate to film and even more difficult to finance.

One-hour dramatic television series (called simply *episodic* television) and half-hour sitcoms are developed in a much different way than long-form movies. They are built around a central concept that provides an inexhaustible source of individual story possibilities. This is usually a *venue* such as a big-city emergency room (*ER*) or a neighborhood bar "where everybody knows your name" (*Cheers*). Within this venue a "home cast" of characters is developed that provides a rich interplay of points of view and character types. Sometimes the venue and cast will be created to showcase a specific star (such as Bette Midler); in other cases the characters are archetypes that may be played by a succession of actors (witness the cast changes in long-running shows like *NYPD Blue* or *Law & Order*). Series development is a highly specialized, complex, and high-risk arena, and networks have separate departments devoted entirely to it. The crucial element in the development of any series is the presence of a writer-producer, or a team of writer-producers and director, who have demonstrated the ability to shape a venue and cast, develop a distinctive performance and shooting style, provide scripts on time, and maintain good relationships with a home cast. The best examples of such teams are the writer, producer, and director behind *The West Wing* (Aaron Sorkin, John Wells, and Thomas Schlamme) and the legendary team of writers and director behind *Cheers*, Glen and Les Charles and James Burrows. These people are called **showrunners**, and they usually rise through the ranks as staff writers and directors of other shows until such time as they are able to break out on their own.

Sources of Film Concepts

The underlying concept for a film may come from three main sources: it may be an original idea of pure fiction; it may be inspired by or directly based on a real event, person, or issue; or it may be adapted from previously published material. Each requires a somewhat different approach.

An original fictional idea for a film may be inspired by a fictionalized view of a historical person or event, as was the film *Gladiator*; it may be inspired by an issue or topic of current interest, as was the film *Network*; or the idea may come from the producer's, director's, or writer's own life, as did Barry Levinson's *Avalon* trilogy.

On the other hand, many films are adapted from previously published material, such as the novel *The Color Purple* or the nonfiction book *The Perfect Storm*. Adapting a book for the screen presents special challenges. For one thing, most books contain a great deal more material than can be contained in a film, and the producer and writer have to decide what to include and what to leave out. This was the challenge facing David O. Selznick when he approached *Gone With the Wind*, and he solved it brilliantly. For another example, when John Irving adapted his own novel, *The Cider House Rules*, he minimized one of the two major characters and story lines, choosing to include only half of the novel.

Another problem of adaptation is that a novelist can take us inside the minds of the characters, making much of the action of most novels "internal." The film producer, writer, and director must decide how to translate this internal action into a cinematic form. There are several ways to do this: the most obvious is the use of voice-over narration as a kind of cinematic soliloquy. When novelist Michael Blake adapted his book *Dances with Wolves*, for example, he used the spoken thoughts of his hero, Lt. Dunbar, as he wrote in his journal. An even better way of expressing inner thoughts on film, however, is the simplest but the most challenging: a skillful writer and director can provide the actors with opportunities to express **subtext**, the unspoken thoughts and attitudes that the camera can capture so well. For example, when Omar Sharif as Doctor Zhivago in David Lean's film wordlessly watches a slaughter of protestors, the camera shows us almost none of the horror, but we "see" it through Zhivago's reaction; we literally read his mind. In such moments, we see why film pioneer D. W. Griffiths once said, "The camera photographs thought."

Films are also adapted from stage plays, such as *The Odd Couple* and *Miss Evers' Boys*. Unlike adapting a novel, adapting a play to film may require an *expansion* of the action beyond what can be presented on a stage. This may involve the creation of new scenes, dialogue, and even characters, all of which must be consistent with the style and intent of the original. Sir Laurence Olivier's film version of Shakespeare's *Henry V* is a classic example, which begins at a performance of the play in the Globe Theatre, then moves grandly into an epic visual rendering of the story.

Many television films, and recently some feature films, are "based on a true story," such as the feature films *Schindler's List* and *The Insider*. A film that remains fairly true to reality is called "based on a true story," whereas one that considerably alters reality is called "inspired by real events." When adapting a true story, the producer and writer must remember that history and biography are not necessarily dramatic. Drama requires that we identify with characters who undergo some kind of change in the course of working through a conflict. These three essential ingredients—*identification, conflict,* and *change*—make the difference between history or biography and drama. They often must be heightened by altering the true story on which the film is based. Moreover, a true story rarely has the structure and focus that is necessary for what Eisenstein called the "connected and sequential" flow toward the emotional climax of a satisfying film; the passage of time must usually be greatly condensed, events must sometimes be rearranged, and some characters must be consolidated or invented.

Changes such as these raise crucial ethical questions. Films such as *Mississippi Burning* and *The Hurricane,* for example, have been criticized for misrepresenting history. The defense against such charges is that the changes were required to meet the demands of drama. However, there is a thin and indistinct line between editorial license driven by the need to dramatize and conscious or unconscious distortions caused by a political or personal bias. It is in dealing with true stories that the ethical responsibility of the producer is most tested: To what extent may the truth be compromised or history altered to produce a successful picture?

Summary

This book describes how a film is created, from conception to screen. Though there are differences in the making of various kinds of films, this book will focus on the underlying principles and processes common to all.

The person most responsible for guiding the filmmaking process from start to finish is the producer, who is the central intelligence of a film project. In each phase of the filmmaking process, the producer tries to keep the project true to its creative essence while making the many compromises that are necessary to best utilize the available resources of time, money, and personnel.

The first function of the producer is to conceive or select the underlying concept or material for the film. The producer must remember that film is more a visual than a verbal medium and that the sequence of a film's images can itself produce new meanings. A cinematic story must be told through a sequence of connected images that lead with unbroken momentum toward the climax.

The underlying concept for a film may be fictitious or it may be inspired by or directly based on a real event, person, or issue. It may also be adapted from previously published material such as a book or play. In deal-

ing with true stories, the ethical responsibility of the producer is most tested: To what extent may the truth be compromised or history altered to produce a successful picture?

NOTES

1. Courtesy of the Producers Guild of America, 6363 Sunset Blvd., Hollywood, CA
   90028.
2. Sergei Eisenstein, *The Film Sense*. Trans. Jay Leyda, Meridian Books (New York,
   1957), p. 4.
3. Ibid.

CHAPTER

2 Options and Rights

If the film's story is entirely fiction, or if it is set far enough in the past, the producer is free to develop the project without further ado. If, however, the idea for the production comes from previously published material or from a living person's life story, the producer will need first to procure complete control over the source material. No financing entity will invest in a project without the guarantee that it will have complete control over the source and complete freedom in adapting the source material to the screen. This freedom is achieved by the purchase of the **rights** to the source material.

Options

There is an old saying in the movie business: "Never use your own money." Producers try to minimize the cost of gaining control of a project's underlying material until a network or studio or some other financing entity has agreed to pay for the procurement of rights and the writing of a script, or for the purchase of a script that has been written on *spec* (speculation). One risky way to do this is to approach a network or studio with the idea for a film without first procuring the rights to the underlying material and suggest that the network or studio procure the rights. If the idea is attractive enough, they may do so, and this is a way for small producers to compete for "big" properties without investing their own money. The risk, of course, is that the idea may be stolen and the property developed by a different producer (and yes, this does happen).

A safer approach is to first achieve control over the underlying material, but to minimize the up front cost of this control. This is done by buying an **option**. This means that in return for a small initial payment, the producer reserves the right (the option) to purchase the rights at some later date. The option fee provides this right for some specified period of time. Options often contain several steps. Any deal that contains a series of steps is called a **step deal**. The first step is the *initial option period* (usually 1 year) during which the producer is given exclusive control of the property. Some option agreements contain a second step called a *setup fee*, paid when a studio or network accepts the project into development. At the end of the initial option period, the producer may renew the option for another year or more. The final step, if exercised, is the actual *purchase* of the rights which requires, of course, payment of the full purchase price. Typically, option fees are 10% of the eventual purchase price per year. The purchase price for a life story or book, depending on the notoriety of the person or book, may range between $30,000 and $200,000 for television; therefore, most television option fees may be from $3000 to $20,000. Feature film rights are often double those for television; therefore, feature option fees range from $6000 to $40,000. There are some books and stories that have been optioned so often that they have generated a good income for their owners even though the films have never been made. I know of one book that has been optioned 12 times over the past 16 years.

The complex area of law dealing with *intellectual property* is a highly specialized field; therefore, options and rights agreements are best negotiated and written by lawyers. Because the services of lawyers are costly, however, most small independent producers do their own temporary option agreements in the form of simple **deal memos** to be replaced later by long-form documents if the movie is actually made. There are several essential qualities of a good option deal memo. It should:

1. Define the property.
2. Define the rights to be granted.
3. Provide exclusive control for a specified period.
4. Provide for an optional renewal period.
5. Specify the purchase price.
6. Allow the option to be assigned to another party.

The first of these points, *defining the property*, is handled differently for life stories than it is for previously published materials; more on this later. For now, let us look at each of the remaining points.

The **rights** to be granted should encompass as many forms of potential broadcast and distribution as possible, including those that may be created as digital, broad band, and internet technology develops in the future. The memo should therefore guarantee rights to:

> . . . all forms of broadcast and theatrical distribution throughout the universe in perpetuity in all languages and media now known or hereafter developed.

Exclusivity is particularly important. No one wants to invest time and effort in a project only to have the same project pop up somewhere else. Even when a producer has the exclusive rights to one source of a story, however, it is not unusual for another project dealing with the same subject but based on a different source to conflict—with deadly results. I once spent a year researching and rewriting a television movie about the theft of atomic materials by the Russian Mafia, with a "loose nuke" falling thereby into terrorist hands; my final draft was submitted for approval in the very week that a feature film on the same subject, *Peacemaker*, opened. That was the end of that, except that I now know a lot about the Russian Mafia and loose nukes.

It is crucial that the option provide the right to *renew* for another year, or more, at the end of the initial option period. It may take 2 years or more to sell an idea, and as long to get it made. Many films have been optioned by a number of producers and studios or networks before finally being made. I recently produced a film for HBO based on Ernest Gaines' novel, *A Lesson Before Dying*. It had been optioned by three different producers at different studios and networks over a 6-year period, and only the last option resulted in actual production.

The option agreement must also specify the eventual *purchase price*. Several different purchase prices may be set for different kinds of productions, with lower figures for television and higher figures for feature use. Alternatively, the purchase price may be tied to the size of the eventual picture's budget.

The producer must be able to *assign* (pass on) the rights to the network or studio when production begins. No studio, network, or financing company is willing to invest in a project until it is assured that the rights will eventually be within its complete control. The option agreement will, therefore, contain language such as this:

> Owner understands that Producer may, in the course of preparing the Production, elect to assign these rights. Such assignment will in no way alter the terms of this agreement.

The *purchase price* is usually paid only when filming actually begins. Networks and studios do not seem to mind spending hundreds of thousands of dollars developing scripts that are never made; in fact, the majority of television scripts developed are never produced, and the mortality rate is even higher in feature films (more on the development process in Chapter 5). Only with the *commencement of principal photography* is there confidence that the film will actually be made; therefore, it is not until this point that the full purchase price is finally paid.

Life Stories

In the case of a life story, the option agreement is made with the individual or individuals whose story is being told. Because contract law is uncomfortable with intangibles, the life story is treated as if it were a tangible object called *the Property*. The person whose story is being told is called *the Owner* of the Property. The rights agreement must clearly define the Property, and will probably contain language such as this:

> The Property: Information about the events and occurrences in the life story of Owner and events to which Owner was a party, and the right to depict Owner in those events.

Perhaps most important, no network or studio will put a project into development that they cannot totally control; thus, the agreement must give the producer total creative freedom in adapting the story to film and must avoid granting any creative approvals to the owner. The agreement will therefore contain language such as this:

> Owner understands the need of producers of motion pictures to fictionalize portions of stories for the purpose of dramatic interest, and that for the same reason characters contained therein may participate in both actual and fictional activities. Producer may include in the Production such actual and/or fictional incidents, scenes, situations, dialogue, events, characters and other material. Producer may, at his sole discretion, employ any actor to portray Owner in the Production.

This language is needed to protect the producer and the financing entity from possible lawsuits. However, if a person has become a celebrity through extensive media coverage (e.g., Mike Tyson or Jackie Onassis) they may be considered to have lost the right to privacy and may be treated in a film without permission as long as the depiction is demonstrably true and not libelous. Of course, they (or their estates if they are deceased) can still choose to sue if they wish.

In practice, the network or studio will purchase insurance against such lawsuits called *Errors and Omissions* (**E & O**) insurance. The producer must provide the necessary rights agreements, and the writer must supply supporting documentation in the form of an **annotated script** that indicates the source of each major event and character. These documents are examined by the E & O insurers, who must be satisfied that substantive lawsuits are unlikely. In some cases, unfortunately, the mere likelihood of a lawsuit, however insubstantial, may be enough to cause abandonment of a project.

Books and Plays

When the underlying material for a film is a book or a play, it is fairly easy to define the property, because a book or play has a tangible form. The agreement will specify rights to the *title*, *plot*, *theme* and *characters*, permission to make *changes* in the material, and permission to *advertise* and *market* the material as a film.

However, rights to books or plays are more complex than life-story rights because of the involvement of the **copyright** laws. The rights protected by copyright are a **bundle**, meaning that many kinds of rights are tied together. The motion picture rights are only one of these rights; the others include publishing, live television, radio, videocassette and DVD, stage, and merchandising. The option agreement for a book or play should contain a literary purchase agreement that "unties" this bundle and seizes the motion picture rights, leaving the rest to the original author. A lawyer's help is essential in creating such an agreement.

A book or play that was published a long time ago may no longer be protected by copyright and is said to be in the **public domain**. There are several authors whose works have recently begun to come into the public domain, and producers stand in line ready to pounce on properties such as Edith Wharton's *The Age of Innocence* or Willa Cather's *My Antonia*. However, the copyright law was changed in 1978 and is undergoing constant revision; determining whether something is in the public domain is no longer as simple as it once was. In general, it is safe to assume that anything published before 1903 is in the public domain, and anything published after 1978 will be in the public domain 70 years after the author's death. Things published between 1903 and 1978, however, may or may not be in the public domain depending on a number of factors, and it is safest to consult a copyright attorney or have a copyright search (costing around $500) done.

The Back-End

The purchase price for rights to a life story, book, or play may include provision for *profit participation*, necessitating that a percentage of the film's profit is paid to the Owner. This is called the **back-end**. Writers, directors, and stars also sometimes get back-end deals that are beyond the residuals guaranteed them by their unions; writers, for example, often get 5% of the net profit, and such a deal is said to include five net **points**.

It is important to know that there are various forms of profit: **net** profit is what is left after all costs of production, studio overhead, financing costs, third-party participations, and distribution have been deducted from the **gross** revenues. The common wisdom is that "there ain't no net." Bookkeeping practices in the movie industry are such that the movie *Batman*, for instance, grossed many millions at the box office but showed a net deficit. Despite the popularity and wide syndication of *The Rockford Files*, James Garner received almost no back-end payments, and director Ridley Scott profited little from the back-end of his classic film, *Blade Runner*. Disputes such as these over the back-end are frequent causes of Hollywood lawsuits.

Because of such cases, major stars and directors often fight to receive gross profit points. This means that their percentage is paid *from the first dollar* with no deductions of any kind. *Batman* lost money because its director and stars had gross profit deals; the more the movie grossed, the greater their back-end payments became, and when these were added to the cost of distribution, the result was an ever-increasing deficit—or so the studio accountants would have us believe.

In between net and gross participation there is something called "adjusted gross profit," which allows certain specific deductions to a certain point or "floor." There are also "hard" and "soft" floors, and more. You can see why all this is best left to lawyers who specialize in entertainment law.

Summary

If the idea for a production comes from some recognizable source—a book, play, or someone's life story—the producer will need to procure the rights to the source material to adapt it to the screen. By buying an option, the producer is given exclusive control of the property for a specified period, in return for a small initial payment. A good option agreement should define the property, define the rights to be granted, provide exclusive control for a specified period, provide a renewal period, specify the purchase price, and allow the option to be assigned to another party.

The total option fee is typically 10% of the eventual purchase price, which may include profit participation called the back-end. Participation may be based on various forms of profit: net, gross, and something in between called adjusted gross. Given its complexity and importance, all this is best left to entertainment lawyers.

CHAPTER

3 Pitching

Once the producer has determined the basic concept for the film and procured any necessary rights, he or she must next find the financing that will move the project through the development of a script and toward production. The steps involved in this process are: first, to determine the essential content and structure of the story and the best way to treat it as a film; next, to determine the best market for the particular story; finally, to make the sales presentation called the **pitch** to potential buyers, such as a network, cable company, studio, or individual financiers.

Preparing for the Pitch

Although the pitch itself will be a highly condensed presentation of the story, a great deal of thought goes into it. The producer must first decide how best to treat the material as a film; he or she must identify the essential story elements and the basic structure of the story. A good first step is to prepare a brief written **synopsis** of the story. The synopsis should forcefully present the essence of the story as it would be treated as a film, stressing its special quality. This brief document is sometimes called simply the **pages**. Besides being good preparation for the pitch, a synopsis can be useful as a "leave-behind," material left for the use of the person hearing the pitch.

Producers with financial backing may opt to hire a writer who will prepare the synopsis and make the pitch, but most self-employed producers do their own pitches and prepare their own pages. Because executives are busy people, the synopsis is best kept as short as possible—only three or four pages in length. "Less is more" at this point, assuming that the right "less" is featured in the pitch. (For an example of a synopsis, see Appendix A.)

A synopsis is not to be confused with a **treatment**. The synopsis is a *selling* document that is designed primarily to engage the buyer's interest by telling an exciting story; a treatment is a *working* document that provides a nearly scene-by-scene exposition of the film, including brief descriptions of the major characters and locations. Although the form of a treatment is narrative, snatches of key dialogue may be included, though sparingly. Treatments may be between 10 and 30 pages long, with 15 a good average.

The Writers Guild (WGA) considers a treatment part of a writer's contractual writing process: current WGA minimum for a feature film treatment is between $20,000 and $32,000, depending on whether the film's budget is low (under $2.5 million) or high (over $2.5 million). The equivalent of a treatment in television is called the "story," and pays between $13,000 and $20,000, depending on the length of the program.

The Hook

Any potential buyer, be it a network or studio executive or an independent financier, must consider the marketing potential of the project. Because publicity campaigns are built on short promotional pieces and posters, a brief, compelling statement that captures the essence of the project is needed. This is the **hook** that will bring an audience to the film—a sentence or two that sums up the special quality of the story. Unfortunately, stories that require lengthy or complex exposition are at a distinct disadvantage in the selling process, as are "character driven" stories that depend on an understanding of the psychology of the major characters. In the case of such a complex story, a short, snappy hook may seem like a trivialization, but it is required nonetheless. The complex and morally ambiguous story of *Miss Evers' Boys*, for example, was given a hook on the poster: "*A government lie. A woman sworn to silence. Everyone knew but the people who mattered most.*" A brief summation of the story may also become the **log line** for the project and can be used to describe it in various lists and reviews. For example, "the death of the American Dream expressed in the rise and fall of a boxing champ who can express himself only through violence" describes Martin Scorcese's *Raging Bull*.

The hook should stress the three dramatic essentials: identification, conflict, and change. For example, I recently sold this movie idea to Showtime: "Kept secret for eighty years, the shameful truth about the worst race riot in our nation's history is uncovered and changes forever the family of one of the survivors." The Tulsa race riot of 1921 had already been the subject of several books, documentaries, and news stories and was being investigated by a government commission. Several producers were pitching the story to various networks and cable companies at the same time; I had to find an approach that set my pitch apart from these others. It was the emphasis on the personal, emotional impact on the family of a survivor that provided the hook, elevated the historical subject to the level of drama, and finally sold the project.

The brief pages I prepared to present this true story were based on extensive research and documentation. It would have been a mistake, however, to bury an executive in research at the outset. The pitch itself only stated that documentation was available and would support the designation "Based on a True Story." This designation is a valuable selling point for a television movie.

In rare cases, a treatment that has been written on "spec" may be used in the selling process. For example, my pitch to Showtime aroused strong interest in the race riot story, but the Showtime production department doubted that it could be made within their budgetary range, given its costly period elements and large production demands. To answer these concerns, I wrote a detailed treatment that provided a feasible way of filming the story. After my treatment had been assessed by the network's production department, and after my documentation was examined to prove the authenticity of the story, Showtime made the commitment to develop the project. Because of the special nature of this particular story, this selling process was unusually complex and took several months—most movies are sold into development on the basis of the pitch and pages alone.

Some film ideas are called **high concept**; these have their own hooks by definition. An example is "a live-action version of a Batman comic"; another is "four old guys in space" (*Space Cowboys*). In films such as these, the concept itself is the essence of the movie, and virtually no additional explanation is needed. Because high concept ideas make a strong association with material that is part of the culture's existing vocabulary, they are immediately recognizable and easy to market. Whether the resultant film will be good or not depends not at all on the concept and entirely on the skill of the filmmakers, but in general, high concept ideas are easier to sell than most others.

Selecting the Market

Although the intrinsic power of the story is important, marketing considerations will be equally important in getting a development deal, and it is important to decide which of the available markets is the right one for a particular project.

The first choice is whether a given story should be a feature film, a network **MOW**, or a **made-for-cable** movie. Network MOWs are usually based on true stories that appeal to women (who comprise the bulk of the TV movie audience) and are typically "smaller" and often domestic in nature (feature film executives sometimes reject an idea as being "too television"). Because TV movies can be made much more quickly than features, they are sometime "ripped from the headlines" and deal with news events or issues of immediate interest. The notorious Amy Fisher scandal, for instance, provoked movies on all three networks, which aired within weeks of one another. In another notorious example, the confrontation between the Federal government and the Branch Davidians in Waco, Texas, was in production even before the tragic fire that ended the standoff.

Feature films, on the other hand, are usually "bigger" stories, both in dramatic and physical scope. The most obvious example is the Hollywood epic with its long and illustrious history, from *The Birth of a Nation* to *Gone With the Wind* to *Star Wars*. In recent years, however, we have seen the advent of computer generated imagery (**CGI**) and the various techniques for creating composite imagery (most notably **green screen** in which actors are filmed in front of a green background which is later replaced electronically). Those techniques have made epic stories such as *Gulliver's Travels* and *The Odyssey* feasible for television.

In addition, a few companies, such as RHI/Hallmark in the United States and Luxe Vide in Italy, have begun to finance large-scale television productions. Movies and **mini-series** (4 or 6 hours presented on two or three nights) such as *Jesus* and *Joan of Arc* are "event programming." They have large budgets, though the American network pays only a portion (*Gulliver's Travel*, for example, cost $28 million, with NBC paying less than one-fourth). In recent years, several cable TV outlets, such as HBO and TNT, have also increased some of their movie budgets to over $10 million and now regularly cast major feature film stars and have high production values.

At the same time, stories that seemed well-suited to television, such as the tobacco industry whistle-blower in *The Insider* or the crusading mother in the Julia Roberts film, *Erin Brockovich*, have begun to appear as feature films (it is still surprising to see a feature film advertised as "Based on a True Story," an appellation once reserved for network MOWs). As a result of all this, the distinction between feature and television material is less clear than it once was.

Demographics

Another way to identify the best potential market for a given project is to consider its **demographics**, the age and economic class of people to whom the project will appeal. Each network or studio has a sense of the general market they wish to reach; for example, CBS once looked for material of interest to older viewers, and TNT featured westerns and other historical, male-oriented stories. As corporations have merged, however, the target markets of many outlets have changed; recently, CBS decided to reach a younger audience and TNT has moved away from historical subjects, changes mandated by new leadership under new corporate owners. Of course, demographics rooted in the business plan of some companies remain constant; The Disney Channel will always focus on stories for kids, and Lifetime will always want female-centered stories; even in these cases, however, there are periodic shifts in emphasis: The Disney Channel, for example, has moved away from traditional Disney fare in favor of high-energy contemporary stories for today's "hip" kids.

Some larger studios and networks have divisions that focus on different markets: Showtime, for instance, sets aside a certain number of its movies each year for their family division; Fox has separate family and kids' channels. "Family" by the way, is defined differently by different companies—The Disney Channel appeals to 12-year-olds and hopes they bring the adults along; the Fox Family Channel appeals to "mom" and does not mind if the kids watch too; HBO 4 Kids is going for younger kids and the interactive web market. Sadly, nowadays almost none of these markets will deal with the "classics" of children's literature, and it was only the star power of Patrick Stewart and Neve Campbell that enabled me to write and produce a modern adaptation of Oscar Wilde's classic, *The Canterville Ghost*. In general, the only common quality of "family" programming today is the absence of nudity and profanity.

Projects that do not seem to fit the needs of a major studio, cable company, or television network may be financed and produced *independently*. This will be discussed in the next chapter.

Agents, Managers, Attachments, and Packaging

A producer may be represented by an **agent**, a **manager**, or a **producer's rep**. An agent submits his or her clients for various jobs and negotiates deals for them; in return, the agent receives, by law, a 10% commission of everything the client makes, except for residual payments. Agents represent actors, directors, and writers as well as producers, and are franchised by SAG, the DGA, or the WGA. "Below-the-line" agents specialize in representing cinematographers, unit production managers, assistant directors, and so on.

Managers are not restricted to an agent's 10% commission and often take 15%, although they involve themselves to a greater degree in the professional and even the personal lives of their clients, helping to build their public image, as well as managing many details of their social lives. (The next time you are awed by the size of a star's salary, consider that their agent gets 10%, their manager 15%, their lawyer 5%, and the government 30%).

A producer's rep is usually a lawyer who specializes in selling independent film projects. He or she will have excellent connections among the people who acquire films for distributors, will travel to festivals and film markets on behalf of their clients, and will make the distribution deal when a film is sold. Anyone involved in independent film production should certainly consider having such a representative.

Although many producers do not see the need for representation of any kind, an agent, manager, or rep can be extremely helpful in getting a film project off the ground in a number of ways. One is by **attaching talent** to a project in the form of a star or hot director; such an attachment is a potentially valuable and sometimes essential step in selling an otherwise difficult project. *Miss Evers' Boys*, for example, was made only because Laurence Fishburne and his manager brought his star power to bear in its behalf. Independent filmmakers will sometimes be able to enlist the aid of a star in making a film happen, as did Matt Damon and Ben Affleck with Robin Williams in *Good Will Hunting*.

A large agency may attempt to attach all or most of a film's core creative team (writer, director, and stars) as a **package**. For my first MOW, NBC's *Mercy Mission*, Creative Artists Agency (CAA) provided the writer, the director, and both stars. For this service, the agency received a packaging fee of 6% of the total budget, with 3% paid "up front" (as part of the production budget) and 3% "deferred to the back-end" (paid out of the profits, if any); some agencies charge as much 5% of the gross receipts as a packaging fee. The clients who are part of a package pay no commission to their agency, so it is advantageous for them to be packaged. However, because of the increased cost to the production, packaging is resisted by studios and networks, who in any case may not want all of the attached elements. As one leading television executive put it, "A package is okay only if there's something good inside."

Pitching

Once the synopsis has been prepared, the target market selected, and any attachments made, the project is ready to be pitched. When pitching, the producer must remember that he or she is selling a product to a potential buyer who hopes to profit from it: The collision of art and commerce has begun in earnest.

Getting an appointment with a creative executive may itself be difficult for those starting out in the business. However, most networks and studios will give almost anyone a fair hearing at some level. Before going in to pitch, it is useful to first check whether a particular story is of potential interest by describing it (the "log line" is enough) over the phone, by letter, or through a representative. It may be that the network or studio already has something similar in development or has ruled out such a story by policy ("we don't do period stories" is a common refrain). Why go through the anxiety of a futile pitch or force an executive to sit through one?

There are a number of styles of pitching, and each person must discover what works best for them. Some producers and writers actually rehearse their pitches, using detailed outlines or notes; some go so far as to tell the story scene-by-scene as a kind of "living treatment." I personally dislike the formality of such approaches and prefer instead to establish a strong personal connection with the buyer then tell the story extemporaneously, hoping that my own enthusiasm for it will infect them. I also think that pitches should be short, perhaps only 3 to 5 minutes: an executive knows within a few minutes whether a story is of interest to them or not. If they want more detail, they will ask for it. Supporting documents, such as photos, books, or documentary films can sometimes be helpful: my Tulsa race riot pitch was accompanied by a book and a documentary film, both of which helped to validate the scope and importance of the story.

The Creative Executive

When pitching, it is best to consider the perspective of the person to whom the pitch is being made. This is the "development executive," also called the **creative executive**. Although this appellation is sometimes an oxymoron, most executives are bright, energetic, knowledgeable people, often with production experience. Establishing good relations with a number of executives at various networks and studios is essential to a successful producing career.

The creative executive will not be able to buy the project on his or her own initiative; he or she must in turn pitch it to upper management. The producer's pitch has to infect the executive with the desire to fight for the project and provide them with the ammunition they need to win that fight; the producer's pages, if well done, may be especially useful in this regard (the synopsis in Appendix A helped sell a movie to CBS).

The producer's relationship with the creative executive will be ongoing, because each executive at a studio or network is assigned to cover certain producers. Once a specific project is taken into development, the creative executive will oversee it throughout its life and will be the liaison between the producer and the studio or network regarding all creative matters. Major decisions such as the choice of writer and director, casting, as well as creative decisions made in the course of production and post-production, must be fed through the creative executive to upper management and back down to the producer.

If it is decided to put the project into development, the development deal will be made by the network or studio **business affairs officer** assigned to the project. Just as the creative executive oversees all the major creative decisions, the business affairs officer will oversee all decisions involving money and contracts, and will negotiate all salaries and credits throughout the life of the project. The producer's relationship with both these executives is critical to an efficient, harmonious production process.

Summary

Once the producer has determined the basic concept for the film and procured any necessary rights, he or she must find the financing to move the project through development and toward production. The producer may begin by writing a synopsis that forcefully presents the essence of the story as a film, and most importantly "the hook," the special quality that will attract an audience.

Choosing the right market is crucial. The first choice is between feature film and television, though the distinction between them is less clear than it once was. Another factor is demographics, the age and economic class of people to whom the project will appeal. Each network or studio has a sense of the general market they wish to reach.

An agent, manager, or rep can help sell a project, sometimes by attaching talent. Some agencies may choose to attach all or most of the core creative team of a project as a package, although this is often resisted by networks and studios.

The pitch is made to a "creative executive" and has to motivate them to fight for the project. Once a project is taken into development, this executive will oversee all creative decisions throughout its life; the business affairs officer will oversee all decisions involving money and contracts. The producer's relationship with these executives will be ongoing and is critical to an efficient, harmonious production process.

CHAPTER
4 Financing

The easiest way to finance a film is to sell the idea to a studio, television network, or cable company by pitching it to a creative executive. Assuming that the pitch is successful, the network or studio agrees to cover most or all of the cost of a script, and a development deal is made. There are other, more difficult and time-consuming methods for financing independent film projects, however, and later in this chapter we examine several.

Studio and Network Production Deals

Major film studios, and most cable television companies, such as HBO, Showtime, and TNT, pay the entire cost of producing their films and own them outright. This is because these entities make most of their money from subscriptions and the exploitation of their holdings (their "library") through domestic and foreign distribution, home video, and sales to other outlets. In one of the most common types of producing deals, the producer who initiated the project is paid a straight producing fee and becomes a "producer for hire," working under the supervision of the network or studio. Such producer fees currently range from $150,000 to $300,000 in television, and $250,000 to $500,000 in feature films. Usually the producer will be granted a back-end participation in the net profit in addition to the fee, although this rarely produces significant income. The producer may be required to assume a limited responsibility for cost overruns caused by his or her actions, typically up to about one third of the fee. If the producer has developed the project to some point before bringing it to the studio and, therefore, has invested money in it, a reimbursement of the producer's costs-to-date may also be negotiated.

Network television movies, on the other hand, are usually financed differently from studio or cable films. Networks make their money by selling advertising during the broadcast of their films, and advertising revenues are not enough to pay the entire cost of producing and broadcasting a movie that will be shown only once or twice. The networks, therefore, need a way to procure movies for limited use while paying only a portion of their cost. They do this by offering outside producers a **licensing deal**.

In a licensing deal, once the script is approved, the network prepares (or the producer submits) an estimated preliminary budget; the network then offers the producer a *licensing fee*, which represents a portion of the assumed total cost of production. This varies depending on the attractiveness and estimated cost of the project, but is currently around $2.6 million to $3.4 million, which represents about 75% of estimated total cost of most network movies. The licensing fee may be increased by **breakage**, meaning that if a particular item in the budget, such as a star's salary, ends up costing more than estimated (that is, if it "breaks" the budget allowance) the network agrees to pay the difference up to a set maximum.

The licensing fee gives the network the exclusive right to broadcast (**run**) the film domestically (within the United States) twice over 4 years, or sometimes three times over 5 years. Because networks are usually not involved in foreign distribution, home video, and other forms of exploitation, they are not interested in owning their films outright. Therefore, the producer retains ownership of all these other rights, and it is from the sale of these rights that the producer hopes to make a profit.

Initially, however, the producer is faced with a **deficit**, the difference between the licensing fee and the actual cost of production. For example, a movie that is assumed to cost $3.6 million may be offered a licensing fee of $2.9 million, leaving a deficit of $700,000. This deficit must be financed by the producer, and this is most often done by selling the foreign rights for theatrical or television release to one of the many companies that specialize in foreign distribution. For this reason, producers try to ensure that the stories and stars in television movies have foreign appeal. They will also sometimes shoot alternate scenes that involve nudity or language that is not acceptable on American TV but attractive for a foreign release. (Conversely, some alternate scenes may be shot that are even *less* strong than American TV allows, for "the airplane version.") Later, when the network has used up its runs or its license has expired, the domestic broadcast rights revert to the producer, who may be able to sell them as well, although they rarely fetch more than $100,000. Some distribution companies will pay a lump sum for *all* future rights (perhaps over $1 million) and are willing to wait 4 or 5 years for the domestic rights to become available.

Producers of licensed network television films are faced with yet another kind of deficit. The network will provide money for the production in stages established by a **schedule of payments**. In between these payments, the producer may be faced with a **cash-flow deficit** that must be made up by interim or "bridge" financing, the cost of which is born by the producer. While this delay may seem odd, much about the way the industry handles money can be understood by considering the interest that is earned by money that has been earmarked for a particular purpose but not yet dispersed. It sits in an interest-bearing account for days or weeks, and the interest it earns is called the **float**. For a large studio or network, the money earned by the float can amount to millions in the course of a year. One network for which I produced insisted on using a bank in Wyoming because it took 2 extra days for checks to clear it, thus increasing the float. (Think about the float the next time your bank puts a 5- or 11-day hold on a check you deposit.)

If the licensing fee plus the sale of rights provides more than the movie actually cost to make, the surplus is the producer's profit. A licensing deal obviously encourages the producer to make the movie for less than the cost that was originally estimated, because any savings will go directly into his or her pocket. It is no wonder that the quality of network movies has sometimes suffered as producers have resorted to extreme cost-cutting measures. Most obviously, much production has moved to Canada and other countries where labor costs are lower and the currency exchange rate is favorable (more on this later).

Until recently, antitrust laws prohibited networks from producing their own movies, because this was seen as monopolistic. These laws have now been eliminated, however, and networks have begun to produce and exploit some of their own films through **in-house production**. In the case of these in-house films, the network pays the total cost of production and retains ownership, with the producer receiving a straight fee, just as with the studios and cable companies. However, television networks need many more films than they can possibly produce, so they still license most of their films from outside producers, but are nowadays insisting on more rights and more creative control.

Independent Financing

Some projects, by their nature, cannot be sold to a studio or network, or the artists involved wish to avoid the inevitable loss of creative control that comes with such sales. In these cases, the film may be made independently. Independent films are some of the most successful artistically, and several have become major box office hits as well. Many more, of course, never find distribution, and the people involved in their creation lose everything they have invested by way of time, energy, and money.

Because **indies** are usually made on television-size budgets, or even much less, they can deal with esoteric stories that need not attract a mass audience. A filmmaker just starting out, or one with an idiosyncratic vision, has a better chance of finding production and creative freedom in the indie world. As a result, the indies have been the spawning ground of many major talents, many of whom were then absorbed into the studio system—for example, Steven Soderbergh (*sex, lies, and videotape*), Robert Rodriguez (*El Mariachi*), and John Singleton (*Boyz N the Hood*). The move up to larger budget studio pictures by successful indie filmmakers does not always produce good results, however. As writer James Agee once said, "Official acceptance is the one unmistakable symptom that salvation is beaten again."[1] For this reason, several independent filmmakers have chosen to retain their creative freedom by staying outside the studio system, most notably Woody Allen, John Sayles, and Henry Jaglom. (For a detailed description of the independent film production process, I recommend Greg Merritt's *Film Production: The Complete Uncensored Guide to Independent Filmmaking*, Lone Eagle Publishing, Los Angeles, 1998.)

It is tremendously time-consuming to arrange independent financing, and it requires ingenuity, *chutzpah*, and persistence that will sorely test the commitment of any filmmaker. One way to finance independently is to **pre-sell** certain foreign territories or home video or rental rights, usually through a broker who specializes in this complex business (and charges a commission of 15%). Depending on the nature of the project and the talent involved, rights to other ancillary sources of income can be pre-sold, such as book or music publishing rights and recording or merchandising rights. In all these cases, a pitch to the appropriate company is required, as is an attractive package of story, director, and stars. These pre-sales are not paid for in cash; instead they take the form of a letter of **guarantee** to distribute the film, video, album, or whatever, when finished. This guarantee must then be taken to a bank and converted into cash (minus, of course, a profit for the bank).

Another form of independent financing is the formation of a group of individual investors who become a limited partnership (**LP**). The successful 1996 film, *Welcome to the Dollhouse*, was made for $700,000 and financed by an LP. Here, the liability of each individual investor ("limited partner") is limited to the amount he or she invests, and their potential profit is likewise limited to the percentage that their investment represents of the total budget. The producer becomes the "general partner" and retains complete control over the project; in return for this control, however, his or her liability is unlimited, and the risk is great. Broadway shows are traditionally financed by LPs, and, like them, a film may be sold at "backer's auditions," where an attractive presentation of the project is made to potential investors. Such a presentation must include an **offering/prospectus**, which includes:

- The film's creative merit: screenplay, stars, director, locations;
- The film's promotable elements: star, genre, hook;
- The proposed financial plan, budget, and proof of the expertise of the producer and other key players;
- The film's sales potential, best expressed by a letter from a reputable distribution company.

Everything in the prospectus should be checked by an attorney, because it is a legally binding document.

Less often, a film may be financed by creating an *"S" corporation* ("S" meaning small), often in a state where corporate fees and taxes are low, such as Nevada or Delaware. A corporation, however, is cumbersome and subject to considerable regulation and legal costs, so this is a viable approach only if the budget of the film is well over $1 million. A limited liability company (**LLC**) is somewhere between a limited partnership and a corporation; the 1994 film *Spanking the Monkey*, made for $200,000, was financed by an LLC.

Assuming that the producer somehow manages to finish the film, or enough of it to give a studio or distributor a sense of its quality, a **negative pickup** may be procured. This means that after screening the film or some portion of it, the studio or distributor agrees to distribute it and to provide enough money to finish or improve it. Films screened at film festivals are often bought in this way, as was *Reservoir Dogs* ($1.5 million) and *The Usual Suspects* ($5.5 million).

Bank loans are another source of funding, but only if the producer already has a distribution guarantee or negative pickup deal in place.

Grants are a free source of financing if the nature of the project appeals to the granting agencies. For example, the 1988 independent feature *Stand and Deliver*, the true story of a group of East Los Angeles high school students working to pass a college placement test in calculus, was shot for $1.37 million, *all* of which came from grants:

- $687,000 from the Corporation for Public Broadcasting and *American Playhouse*;
- $350,000 from the ARCO corporation;
- $172,000 from the National Science Foundation;
- $50,000 from the Ford Foundation;
- $50,000 from Pepsi and Anheuser-Busch for product placement.

It took the producer a year of hard, full-time work to accumulate these grants, but the film grossed more than $20 million and resulted in an Academy Award nomination for star Edward James Olmos.[2]

There are other ingenious methods of independent film financing. Author Greg Merritt lists some:

> Methods of raising money are limited only by your imagination . . . whether it be Robert Rodriguez allowing a research center to conduct medical experiments on him in order to forage the funds to make *El Mariachi*, Michael Moore staging bingo games to help finance *Roger & Me*, or Robert Townsend and his *Hollywood Shuffle* credit card collection.
>
> The key is in keeping your costs down. *"Clerks* was made for $27,000 because it was shot in the convenience store that employed writer/director

Kevin Smith. *The Brothers McMullen* was produced for $24,000 in filmmaker Ed
Burns' family house with his mom doing the 'catering.' "[3]

We need not mention *The Blair Witch Project*, which cost $22,000 and grossed
over $140 million in U.S. theaters alone. The advent of digital video film-
making has made low-cost production even more possible, and this will be
discussed in the final chapter.

Regardless of the way in which initial financing is arranged, and
regardless of the size of the budget, the producer will be wise to purchase a
completion bond that will cover cost overruns up to 100% of the original
budget. For this insurance, the bonding company will charge 4% of the total
budget, but it will first have to be convinced of the viability of the project
and the skill of its producers. The budget (which must include a 10% contingency), shooting schedule, track records and reliability of the actors, producer, director, and unit production manager (UPM), will be carefully examined. If it is not satisfied, the bonding company may require the producer to
hire a reliable UPM, or may even, in dire cases, step in and take over the production if necessary.

Film financing is a complex issue. For further information, I suggest
Greg Merritt's book, already mentioned, and also:

- John W. Cones, *43 Ways to Finance Your Feature Film*, Southern Illinois
  University Press, Carbondale, 1995.
- Renee Harmon, *The Beginning Filmmaker's Business Guide*, Walker and
  Company, New York, 1994.
- Paul A. Baumgarten, Donald C. Farber, Mark Fleisher, *Producing,
  Financing, and Distributing Film*, Limelight Editions, New York, 1992.

Summary

A studio or cable company will pay the entire cost of development and production and will then own the film outright. A television network, on the
other hand, will offer a licensing fee that covers only a portion of the estimated cost of production; the producer must find a way to finance the deficit,
usually by selling the foreign distribution rights. Although networks have
recently been allowed to produce some films "in-house," they still license
most of their films from outside producers.

Some projects fall outside the established markets and may be produced and financed independently by pre-selling certain territories or rights.
These pre-sales result in letters of guarantee that must be taken to a bank
and converted into cash. A filmmaker may also form a group of individual
investors who become a limited partnership (LP). Less often, a film may be
financed by a small "S" corporation. If the producer somehow manages to

finish all or most of the film, a negative pickup deal may be procured. Bank loans are another source of funding, as are grants if the nature of the project appeals to the granting agencies. However the project is financed, the producer will be wise to purchase a completion bond to cover possible cost overruns.

NOTES

1. James Agee and Walker Evans, *Let Us Now Praise Famous Men*, Houghton Mifflin, Boston, 1941, p. 4.
2. Greg Merritt, *Film Production: The Complete Uncensored Guide to Independent Filmmaking*, Lone Eagle Publishing, Los Angeles, 1998, p. 28.
3. Greg Merritt, *Film Production: The Complete Uncensored Guide to Independent Filmmaking*, Lone Eagle Publishing, Los Angeles, 1998, p. 30.

CHAPTER

5 Development Hell

All development and producing deals contain **contingencies**, certain conditions that must be met before the project will be allowed to proceed to production. Usually, the network or studio will require (in this order) approval of the *writer, script, budget, director,* and one or two *lead actors*. Only when all these contingencies have been met is the **green light** (the order to begin production) given. Each of these steps requires a lengthy process of decision-making and negotiations, so the development process can take anywhere from 8 months to 2 years, and the outcome is always uncertain. No wonder those in the industry commonly refer to this as "**development hell**."

As an example of how the development decision-making process works, consider the first major choice to be made after a project has been taken into development—the hiring of the writer. The creative executive works with the producer to develop a list of potential writers who are of mutual interest; the producer then checks the availability of each by calling their agents; the executive and the producer then prioritize the list of those available; the executive then applies to upper management for approval of perhaps three possibilities. Upper management may or may not agree with the priorities on the original list, and may even suggest entirely different names; the producer is then empowered to make an offer to the first writer on the approved list. The producer contacts the writer's agent and presents the project, and if the writer is interested, an offer is made.

In a network licensing deal, the network business affairs officer will give the producer a figure that the network is prepared to "recognize" within the licensing deal; this is almost always less than what the writer has most recently been paid (the writer's **quotes**) and the producer will have to supply the difference. For example, I recently hired a writer whose lowest recent quote was $95,000 plus a **production bonus** (an additional fee paid if the film is actually made) of $37,500; the network recognized only $88,500 toward the fee and $30,000 toward the bonus, meaning that I had to supply the $15,000 difference from my profit (if any). It also means that if the project is abandoned without being made, I will lose the $7500 I am contributing toward the writer's basic fee. In a licensing deal, the deficit begins even before the producer is sure of any income!

The first writer who is approached may not agree to take on the project, or may reject the terms offered. If necessary, the whole process is repeated with the second name on the list and so on, until a writer is finally hired.

The Writing Process

The writer's deal is made in steps with a portion of the total compensation paid at the conclusion of each step. Three basic steps are defined by the WGA: The treatment (called the "story" in television), the first draft, and the final draft. In practice, additional steps may be added by negotiation. The final draft, for instance, may be followed by a **polish**, for which an additional fee may be paid. Most writing deals include a production bonus; some also contain a back-end, typically five points of net. Both the production bonus and the back-end are reduced if subsequent writers are hired.

Once the writer has been hired, the producer, creative executive, and writer meet to discuss the story and to share ideas. If the consensus coming from this meeting is strong, the first step of treatment or story may be waived, and the writer goes off to work on the first draft; otherwise, a treatment is required and, when finished, is submitted for approval. Sixteen or so weeks later, the first draft is delivered, going first to the producer. At this point, the producer may ask the writer to make some modest changes before submitting it to the creative executive, but such additional writing, while common, is technically against WGA rules.

Within 21 days after the draft is submitted, the creative executive gives his or her **notes**. Notes may be delivered in writing, although a face-to-face meeting or telephone conference call is held to discuss them and exchange ideas. This process continues through each step of the writing deal until the final draft is submitted; the creative executive then sends it to upper management for final approval. It is not uncommon for upper management to then issue yet another set of notes. If the script is still not approved after the notes on the final draft have been executed, the writer's deal may be extended for another draft, or, more commonly, another writer will be hired to do a rewrite.

Rewrites are often done to address certain aspects of a script, and, therefore, some writers specialize in fixing dialogue, others in heightening character, yet others in clarifying structure. Given this sort of "assembly line" approach by studios with a lot of money to spend on writers, it is not uncommon for six or seven writers to work on a feature film. In television, the amount of rewriting is much less, although a script may often be "punched up" by another writer. The WGA will currently not permit more than three writers to receive credit on any one project, no matter how many have actually worked on it.

The Writers Guild makes an effort to protect the work and credit of the original writer, but it is caught in a dilemma: Most of the paid writing work in Hollywood is for rewrites, and there is sharply divided opinion among writers about how subsequent writers should be recognized for their contributions. Under current rules, each new writer must be informed of any prior writers, and a rewriter will not usually receive any credit unless it can be shown that they have significantly changed the fundamental structure of the piece or rewritten a large percentage of it. The determination of writing credit is always made by the Writers Guild itself, often through a process of **arbitration** in which copies of the various versions of the script are examined by a randomly chosen panel of three anonymous writers.

Copyright and Registration

The producer and writer both have reason to want as much protection against the theft (**plagiarism**) of their material as possible. This is achieved by **copyrighting** the material. Under U.S. law, "any original work of authorship written in this country since January 1, 1978, is automatically protected under U.S. copyright when it is fixed in a tangible medium of expression." An "original work of authorship" can be a script, treatment, or even a synopsis, although an idea or a title cannot be copyrighted. Being "fixed in a tangible medium" simply means being written down, recorded, photographed, and so on.

Under current copyright law, works are covered whether or not a copyright notice is attached and whether or not the work is registered with the copyright office. However, most scripts display the copyright symbol and date (©2000), and it is still a good idea to **register** material with the copyright office, which will provide the necessary forms on request. Another way to register material is by depositing a copy with the Writers Guild and paying a modest fee ($15 for nonmembers); this service is available to anyone.

Copyrighting and registering should be standard practice for every writer, but even then there is no sure defense against plagiarism. Because an idea may occur to several people at once, plagiarism is almost impossible to prove unless there is a "paper trail" that shows an idea has been exposed to someone who later appropriated it. This happened in the famous case between Art Buchwald and Paramount Pictures. Buchwald had sold a treatment of a story to Paramount about an African king who comes to New York and finds a wife in Queens. The project was put into development and the first script was written by Buchwald's partner Alan Bernheim. Besides their fees, Buchwald and Bernheim were promised points of the picture's net profits, should it be made. Subsequent writers were hired to do rewrites, but after spending over half a million on scripts, the Paramount executives who bought the project moved to other studios, and Paramount dropped the project. Buchwald and Bernheim then sold the project to Warner Brothers, but shortly thereafter Paramount made a film starring Eddie Murphy called *Coming to America* that seemed to be so similar to Buchwald's idea that Warner Brothers dropped the project. When Buchwald saw *Coming to America* in a little theater on Martha's Vineyard, he was amazed to discover that it was, in fact, based on his material. He filed suit, and after a costly court battle, Buchwald and Bernheim were awarded their net profits. Paramount determined that these profits amounted to $900,000, a sum that did not even cover Buchwald's legal costs and was a small fraction of the film's gross of $350 million. Nevertheless, Buchwald considered the judgment to be a moral victory. There was hope for a time that Buchwald's crusade might change the way business is done in Hollywood, but of course it didn't.

To be fair to the studios, it is true that almost every successful feature film provokes a number of claims of plagiarism, and often these "nuisance lawsuits" are settled by negotiated payments because they would cost more to fight in court. For this reason, producers and studios will accept scripts and treatments only from registered agents or attorneys or from writers willing to sign a release that forgoes any future claim of plagiarism.

The Preliminary Board and Budget

Once the script has been given final approval, a new person joins the team. This is the studio's or network's **production executive**. Like the creative executive and business affairs officer, the production executive will remain with the project throughout its life, supervising all aspects of physical production. This person's first task is to oversee the creation of a *preliminary budget*. The approved script is given to a member of the production department who is called an **estimator**, or it is jobbed out to a unit production manager (UPM) or "**line producer**" (more on them later). This person first does a **breakdown** of the script, scene-by-scene, to identify the various locations, the size of the various roles, and the most costly elements such as extensive night shooting, period sets and costumes, crowds, children, rain, special vehicles, animals, effects, special construction needs, special equipment, and so on. From this breakdown, a preliminary **board** is created, which suggests how many days of shooting the script will require, how long the various actors will work, and so on (more on boards later). From this preliminary board, the estimated budget is created.

Film budgets are divided by an imaginary line: the costs **above-the-line** are the cost of the "creative" components of the film, and include:

- The story costs for rights and writer;
- Producer fees and costs;
- Director fees and costs;
- Cast fees and costs;
- Agent fees;
- Fringe benefits for the above-the-line personnel.

The remaining "technical" costs of the production are all **below-the-line**. The below-the-line portion of the budget is divided into three main areas that cover the production period, the post-production period, and "total other" charges such as legal fees. Each production department has a section and reference number of its own, and the line-by-line details of the budget are summarized on the **top sheet** (see Figures 5.1 and 5.2). At one time, the total cost of a film was about one third above-the-line and two thirds below, but the salaries of major stars today can make it closer to half and half.

The total cost established by the estimated budget is then considered by the network or studio. At this point, certain cost-cutting measures may cause alterations in the script. Some of the most common ways of reducing the cost of a film are:

- Reduce the number of shooting days, probably by making cuts in the script to shorten it.
- Consider shooting in a state or country where costs are lower.
- Reduce the number of locations by consolidating some, eliminating others. One of the most important ways to save time (and, therefore, money) is to avoid moving the company, at least in the course of a working day.
- Avoid costly night shoots by changing night scenes to day scenes wherever possible.
- Avoid large crowd scenes.
- Avoid rain, fire, animals, and, especially, children.
- Consider using **stock footage** to replace certain shots.
- Consider using **mattes** or other forms of composite imagery to reduce construction costs.

The use of computer generated imagery (**CGI**) can save money by reducing construction and location costs, but only if the movie is to be delivered in video; if the show must be delivered on film, CGI will probably not cut costs because transfer of CGI to film is very expensive (currently around $1.75 per frame, though this cost will lessen as technology advances).

Based on the preliminary budget estimate, costs may be cut to the point in which the essence of the movie is threatened, but if the budget is

"I'll Never Try This Again"
2 HOUR Movie of the Week (Network)

Exec. Producer: Mona Lott & Titus A. Fist   Schedule: 22 days - Location
Producer: George Speldin   Script dated: 6/27/1984
Director: Alan Smithee
35mm. Film Stock: Film/Video Finish   Daily work hrs.: 11 shoot + 1 prep/wrap
WGA/SAG/DGA/IA/Teamster   Wardrobe & Teamsters: 11 + 2 prep/wrap
Preliminary Budget #1 (rev)   Prepared by: Anne Other
                                                   Date: April 1, 1999

Acct#	Category Title	Page	Total
1100	STORY, RIGHTS & CONTINUITY	1	$152,400
1200	PRODUCERS	1	$470,424
1300	DIRECTOR	1	$104,320
1400	CAST	1	$1,258,605
1500	TRAVEL & LIVING COSTS	2	$113,345
1900	**ATL FRINGES**		**$54,059**
	Total Above-The-Line		**$2,153,153**
2000	PRODUCTION STAFF	3	$278,259
2100	EXTRA TALENT	5	$56,965
2200	SET DESIGN	6	$83,150
2300	SET CONSTRUCTION	6	$87,200
2500	SET OPERATIONS	6	$110,709
2600	SPECIAL EFFECTS	8	$29,000
2700	SET DRESSING	8	$108,673
2800	PROPERTY	9	$75,784
3000	WARDROBE	10	$147,349
3100	MAKEUP & HAIR	11	$55,398
3200	LIGHTING	12	$71,132
3300	CAMERA	13	$127,760
3400	PRODUCTION SOUND	14	$35,505
3500	TRANSPORTATION	15	$242,758
3600	LOCATIONS	18	$319,629
3700	FILM & LABORATORY	20	$146,062
3900	**BTL FRINGES**		**$247,982**
	Total Production		**$2,223,315**
4500	FILM EDITING	21	$102,125
4600	MUSIC	21	$40,500
4700	POST PRODUCTION SOUND	21	$65,110
4800	POST-PROD. FILM & LAB.	22	$70,350
4900	MAIN & END TITLES	22	$12,500
5900	**POST FRINGES**		**$22,621**
	Total Post Production		**$313,206**
6700	INSURANCE	22	$44,635
6800	GENERAL EXPENSE	23	$40,000
			$0
	Total Other Costs		**$84,635**
	TOTAL ABOVE-THE-LINE		**$2,153,153**
	TOTAL BELOW-THE-LINE		**$2,621,156**
	TOTAL ABOVE & BELOW-THE-LINE		**$4,774,308**
	GRAND TOTAL		**$4,774,308**

FIGURE 5.1   A budget top sheet. This hypothetical budget created by Derek Kavanagh.

Acct#	Description	Amount	Units	X	Rate	Subtotal .	Total
3200	**LIGHTING**						
3201	Rigging						
	LOCAL						
	ALLOWANCE		Allow		3,500	3,500	$3,500
3203	Gaffer						
	LOCAL						
	PREP	11	P.HRS	5	22.66	1,246	
	SHOOT	14	PHRS	19	22.66	6,028	
	SATURDAYS	18	HRS	3	22.66	1,224	
	WRAP	11	P.HRS		22.66	249	$8,747
3204	Best boy electric						
	LOCAL						
	PREP	11	P.HRS	3	19.57	646	
	SHOOT	14	PHRS	19	19.57	5,206	
	SATURDAYS	18	HRS	3	19.57	1,057	
	WRAP	11	P.HRS		19.57	215	$7,124
3205	Operating labor						
	LOCAL						
	ELECTRIC #1						
	PREP	11	P.HRS	2	17.51	385	
	SHOOT	14	PHRS	19	17.51	4,658	
	SATURDAYS	18	HRS	3	17.51	946	
	WRAP	11	P.HRS		17.51	193	
	ELECTRIC #2						
	PREP	11	P.HRS	2	17.51	385	
	SHOOT	14	PHRS	19	17.51	4,658	
	SATURDAYS	18	HRS	3	17.51	946	
	WRAP	11	P.HRS		17.51	193	
	ELECTRIC #3						
	SHOOT	14	PHRS	19	17.51	4,658	
	SATURDAYS	18	HRS	3	17.51	946	
	WRAP	11	P.HRS		17.51	193	$18,161
3216	Purchases						
	EXPENDABLES	22	Days		300	6,600	$6,600
3217	Equipment rentals						
	PACKAGE	4	Weeks		5,500	22,000	
	ADD'L FOR NIGHT		Allow		3,500	3,500	$25,500
3248	Loss & damage						
	CHARLOTTE		Allow		500	500	$500
3285	Other Costs						
	BOX RENTAL						
	GAFFER	4	Weeks		250	1,000	$1,000
						Total For 3200	**$71,132**

FIGURE 5.2   A budget detail

still more than the money available, the entire project will be abandoned. In a licensing deal, if the licensing fee plus the sale of rights adds up to less than the estimated budget, the producer may have to walk away from years of work rather than risk losing money; sadly, networks often put producers in this position.

Runaway Production

As the cost of production has gone up, producers, networks, and studios have looked for ways to cut costs, especially the very high daily cost of shooting. The cost of shooting is different in various places because of differences in local wage scales and work regulations, currency exchange, and the possibility of governmental inducements such as tax breaks; as a result, some places are more cost-effective for film production than are others. At one time, certain "right-to-work" states, where unions were less powerful, were popular film locations. Georgia, North Carolina, and Florida were especially popular, and a pool of local actors and crews, along with an infrastructure such as equipment rental houses, film labs, film truck rental companies, and caterers, gathered to support the local film industry in those areas. In recent years, however, the various film unions have negotiated national agreements with most producers, so the financial incentive offered by these "right-to-work" states has been greatly reduced and film production has moved even further away.

Today, more films are made outside the United States than in it, and **runaway production** is the single greatest concern of Americans working in the film and television industry. Great Britain, Ireland, Mexico, and Australia have attracted considerable numbers of American films. Of all foreign locations, however, Canada is by far the most attractive because of its proximity, lower labor costs, less restrictive work regulations, tax incentives, and very favorable rate of currency exchange. At any given time, there may be more than 30 films being shot in Toronto and 25 to 30 in Vancouver. Some television outlets make nearly all their movies in Canada and have Canadian corporations set up to handle their production needs. At the same time, the Canadian government and local unions have placed limits on the talent that can be imported to work on films; often, only the producer, director, and a star or two is imported, and the rest of the cast and crew must be hired locally. This has placed a severe strain on Canadian talent pools, while thousands of qualified American actors and craftspeople remain unemployed in Hollywood. American film unions, a number of states, and the federal government are all considering incentives to lure production back home, but so far none have been effectively implemented.

It is a challenge to create a believable sense of place when shooting in a locale other than the one required by the script. Toronto, for example, has doubled as New York, Washington, DC, New Orleans, Atlanta, Los Angeles, Viet Nam, London, and many other places. **Establishing shots** taken from **stock footage**, second-unit work when affordable, and ingenious art direction may help to some degree, but because the best reason for shooting on location is added realism, quality inevitably suffers. As usual, however, the financial considerations outweigh all these shortcomings.

Hiring the Director

After the script and the preliminary budget have been approved, the last of the contingencies remain to be met: the director and stars must be hired. No matter how much has been spent to bring the project to this point, it is only a small fraction of the eventual total cost of production, so the project will be abandoned if the desired talent cannot be procured (and remember that the producer has so far made nothing).

Sometimes, a director will have been involved with a project during its development, but usually the director is hired only after the script has been approved. The same process used to hire the writer is used to hire the director: lists are prepared, availabilities checked, approvals given in order of priority, and offers made.

Offers to directors are always **reading offers**, meaning that the director's agent will first negotiate an acceptable fee, billing, and **perks** (perquisites). Perks are special requirements regarding accommodations on and off the set, exclusive transportation, special assistants, makeup and hair persons, and other things that can have an enormous impact on the budget. Only when these negotiations are concluded does the director read the script and decide whether to accept the assignment or not. Each reading offer usually takes a minimum of a week and as long as a month to work itself out.

Once the director is hired, something close to a second development process begins as he or she shapes the script for actual shooting. The writer may or may not be involved in this process, although in the best of circumstances they are; the WGA hopes to make the writer's involvement mandatory throughout the production process. Even when this happens, however, the writer has limited influence: studios and networks tend to respect the creative ideas of directors and stars above those of writers and producers, because directors and stars have more power to impede production and attract audiences.

Star Casting

As soon as the script and budget have been approved for production, a **casting director** joins the team. Most studios and networks have their own casting people on staff, though an additional casting director is always hired to handle the myriad details of the casting process. The greatest value of a good casting director is his or her up-to-date knowledge of a wide variety of actors, including not only the roles they can play, but also their reliability and cooperativeness.

The casting of stars is as much an economic as a creative decision. The producer must provide one or two stars for the leads, who, in the opinion of the network or studio, will attract a sufficient audience to justify the cost of production and distribution. Banks and financing companies that specialize in financing films have their own ideas about the value of various actors (one actor may be more "bankable" than another), and networks and cable companies have their own ideas about which actors are best for their particular audience. The value of an actor or director in the foreign market must also be considered; directors, by the way, tend to be more highly valued by Europeans than by Americans, a sign of the greater sophistication of the European audience.

Stars must give their approval not only of the script, but also of the director. Auditions for lead roles are rarely held, because a star is not usually expected to audition. It is big news when stars do audition because of their desire for a role or because they want to work with a particular director, as when Tom Cruise and Nicole Kidman auditioned for Stanley Kubrick for *Eyes Wide Shut*.

After much discussion between the producer, director, and creative executive, an agreement is reached about possible stars acceptable to all. A short list of perhaps three possible actors in order of preference is created for each leading role. Starting with the first name, a reading offer is made by the casting director to the actor's agent. Because most stars are considering a number of offers at any given time, many offers are refused, and often several actors must be approached before a deal is closed. Each actor may take several weeks to read the script before deciding, so it usually takes many months to complete the process of star casting. I once produced a cable television film, for instance, in which the lead role was offered to 17 actors before the star was finally hired, a process that took 6 excruciating months during which the entire project was in constant jeopardy.

The situation is worsened by the fact that stars and established directors will consider only **pay or play** offers, meaning that the artist will be paid even if the film is not made. For weeks and months, the network or studio tries to hang on to talent while avoiding commitment to pay or play deals until all elements are in place. This period is sometimes called "the flashing green light" because projects have sometimes been abandoned even after costly pay or play deals have been made.

Only when the stars are set does the show get the final green light. Now the principal supporting roles, usually three to six in number, are cast to round out the **marquee** of the show. These roles are usually played by well-established actors, so auditions are held only if there is some question about the choice and the actor is willing.

Billing

Credit, also called **billing**, is an especially delicate area of negotiation. Film credits are divided into two sections: The **main title sequence** appears at the beginning of the picture (although in feature films they sometimes appear at the end to avoid disrupting the start of the story). The **end credits** are the so-called "technical" credits, although in truth you will find many essential creative people listed here.

The title sequence contains the main financial and creative credits. First come the **company credits** of the financing entity or entities, and the complexity of film financing is often reflected in these, such as:

Universal
and Paramount Pictures
in Association with Canal Plus
and Two Cities Entertainment present
an Anglo-Amalgamated/Zodiac Production of . . .

Each name or set of names constitutes a **card** (from the days when credits were literally shot from typeset boards) and a "single" card is preferable to a "shared" card.

After the company credits, usually, comes the "possessory" credit for the director, such as "An Allen Smithee Film." This credit, by the way, is resented by writers (the WGA calls it the "vanity" credit) and is currently the subject of considerable debate; the WGA made its elimination a point of negotiation for its industry-wide contract, much to the displeasure of the Directors Guild (DGA).

Next are the **above the title** credits for the major stars. The title itself establishes the size of the typeface for all other credits, which are by contract stated to be "100% of the title," or some lesser size. After the title, the other principal actors are listed in descending order of importance (or descending order of the clout of their agents); it is a delicate aspect of negotiation to keep billing options open as various actors are promised their position in the billing. The supporting actors come next, often sharing cards. Next, special credits for **cameo** appearances may be indicated by a credit such as "with George Spelvin as Uncle Jack." ("George Spelvin" and "Alan Smithee," by the way, are traditional fictitious names used when actors and directors, respectively, do not want their real names to appear.)

After the principal actors, the key creative credits begin. From this point on, the most important credits are those closest to the end of the sequence, that is, closest to the start of the story. For this reason, the DGA requires that the last credit in the main title sequence must be that of the director, and the WGA demands that the next-to-last credit be the writer (and in an adaptation, the material on which the film is based).

The credit just before the writer will be the primary producer. This credit is sometimes shared by more than one person; if they are a team, their names may be listed together on a shared card. In MOWs and series television, the primary producer will sometimes be given the "freeze frame" credit at the very end of the story, just before the end credits begin. (For an example of main title credits, see Appendix B.)

The first end credit is usually a complete list of the cast by character and actor name. The DGA requires that the first card after the cast is shared by the Unit Production Manager and Assistant Directors. After that, there is no standard sequence of end credits, although each network or studio may have its own preferred form.

Abandonment, Turnaround, and Reversion

There are many reasons why a project may be abandoned before it reaches production. The script and subsequent rewrites may not have been acceptable, the estimated budget may have been too high, the desired casting may have been impossible, or—frequently in television—a change in the management of the network or studio may cause a change in the type of movie desired. This last is a special concern for producers. Projects remain in development for long periods of time and changes in management happen fairly frequently in the industry; when a new management moves in, it usually drops many of the projects already in development. The reasoning is simple: If the new management makes an old project and it is successful, the credit will go to the previous management; if it is unsuccessful, the blame will go to the new management.

When a project is abandoned, the network or studio, because it has paid for whatever writing has been done, owns the script. It may, however, grant the producer a **turnaround**. When a project goes "into turnaround," the producer is given the opportunity to sell it elsewhere; if he or she is successful, the original studio or network is immediately repaid all its costs plus interest and may retain some credit and profit participation. Many famous films were developed at one studio, then put into turnaround and moved to a second studio, as was Steven Spielberg's *E.T.* Many film studios resist granting turnarounds because they look foolish if they drop a project and it is later successful elsewhere, so a turnaround provision must be negotiated in advance and should be part of any producing deal.

Even without a turnaround, the WGA Basic Agreement requires that at some point the script can revert to the writer's (not the producer's) control. This is called *separated rights*. You already know that copyright protects a "bundle" of rights; the WGA has negotiated to separate some of these rights to be reserved by the writer. After a prolonged period of inactivity on an unproduced script (4 years in television and 5 in feature films) the writer may apply to regain sufficient control to try to sell the script elsewhere; if the writer is successful, the original network or studio is repaid. If the writer is unsuccessful, the project reverts back to the studio or network and is, for all practical purposes, dead.

Summary

In a development deal, the network or studio will set contingencies that must be met before the green light is given: these are (in order) approval of the writer, script, budget, director, and one or two lead actors. The period during which these contingencies are being met is commonly referred to as "development hell."

The first task in development is the hiring of the writer. A writing deal will have at least three basic steps: the treatment or "story," the first draft, and the final draft. After each draft, the producer and creative executive give notes. The final draft is sent to upper management for final approval. Rewrites are sometimes ordered, and the determination of writing credit is always made by the Writers Guild, often through a process of arbitration. To protect material and prove when it was written, it should always be copyrighted and registered.

Once the script has received final approval, the production executive oversees the creation of a preliminary budget from a breakdown of the script and a preliminary board. Film budgets are divided with creative components "above-the-line," and the remaining technical costs "below-the-line."

After the budget is approved, a director is hired and shapes the script for shooting. A casting director helps select the stars and pay-or-play reading offers are made. When the stars have been set, the show gets the green light and principal supporting roles are cast to round out the "marquee."

Billing is divided between the main title sequence, in which the last credit must be that of the director, next-to-last the writer, and before that the primary producer. The end credits are the "technical" credits.

When a project is abandoned, the network or studio owns the script, although it may grant the producer a turnaround. At some point, the writer may apply for separated rights.

CHAPTER

6   Prep

There are two main camera formats in common use: the three-camera and the single-camera. The three-camera format, in which several cameras run simultaneously from different angles, offers the advantage of speed and the ability to shoot large sections of material in a more or less finished form. Although more general lighting is necessary and camera placement is restricted, the three-camera format is the best way to capture the living presence of an ensemble performance, and it is used for all television sitcoms and soap operas. This format is discussed in Chapter 9.

The single-camera format is much slower and more costly than the three-camera, but it allows more subtle creative control. It is used in all feature films, television movies made for network or cable, and episodic television dramas such as *ER* and *NYPD Blue*. The most striking aspect of single-camera film production is that shooting is piecemeal—each scene or portion of a scene rehearsed, staged, and shot at one time, although seldom in chronologic sequence. To understand this unique aspect of single-camera film production, one must first understand how the shooting of a single-camera film is organized.

The Schedule

The production of all films is divided into three periods: the preparation, or **Prep**, the **Shoot** itself, and the period of postproduction, or **Post**. The Prep will usually be slightly longer than the Shoot itself, and the Post will be roughly twice as long as the Prep and Shoot combined. Of the three periods, the Shoot is always the shortest because it is by far the most expensive on a daily basis; a feature film shooting on location costs between $100,000 and $150,000 per day, a television film about one third less. The length of the Shoot is called simply the **schedule** and is measured in days, as in a "24-day schedule." The longer the schedule, the greater the chance for quality work because the number of script pages to be shot per day is reduced, allowing more complex camera setups and lighting, more rehearsal, and more takes.

The various kinds of film production have different typical shooting schedules. For example, network television one-hour episodic dramas such as *Law and Order* or *The West Wing* have a budget anywhere from $1 million to over $13 million per episode (a record set by *ER* in 2000), and an episode will be shot in 7 or 8 days (about seven script pages per day); one episode is being shot while another is in Prep and yet another is in Post.

The average network television movie has a budget that is between $3 million and $6 million, and an overall production period of 18 to 20 weeks; it will Prep for 4 or 5 weeks, Shoot for 19 to 22 days (about four or five pages a day), and Post for 10 or 12 weeks.

A high-quality made-for-cable television movie costs between $5 million and $12 million; it has an overall production period of 20 to 24 weeks. It will Prep for 5 or 6 weeks, Shoot for 22 to 30 days (three or four pages a day), and Post for 16 or more weeks.

A theatrical feature film made by a major studio has a much larger budget, ranging from $20 million to $180 million and a correspondingly longer production period. It will Prep for months and Shoot for 60 or more days, completing only a page or two of script each day, and it may Post as long as 26 weeks. Some feature films exceed this: Sydney Pollack's *Out of Africa* prepped for a year and shot for more than 100 days; *Pearl Harbor* is rumored to cost over $200 million.

Independent feature films that are made outside the studio system are often made with budgets and schedules that are similar to those of television movies, and sometimes much less. They are organized and shot in a similar way, but on a more modest scale and with a much looser organization, with fewer people each doing a variety of jobs.

Despite these differences, the production process is the same for all types of single-camera films—only the scale of the undertaking differs. What follows, then, will describe the organizational principles that are common to network, made-for-cable, studio, or independent movies.

The Line Producer and UPM

As soon as a project has been given the green light, one of the most important people on any movie set joins the team (although it is likely that he or she has already been involved in preparing the preliminary budget). This person is the **line producer** or unit production manager (**UPM**). Line producers and UPMs are responsible for determining the final budget and then controlling that budget throughout the production process. They handle the manifold details of production: hiring and firing personnel; observing union regulations; arranging equipment, transportation, and housing deals; keeping track of costs through daily production and cost reports; and the thousand other things that make a film company function. No one has to know more about film production than a line producer or UPM; he or she is involved in the operation of every department and all phases of the filmmaking process.

The difference between a line producer and a UPM is basically one of rank. A UPM is responsible for all the organizational and logistical details mentioned above but has little creative involvement in the actual content of the show. A line producer does all this (having had considerable prior experience as a UPM) but has a greater degree of creative involvement and responsibility as well. Line producer is therefore a more prestigious credit and often appears in the main titles, whereas the UPM is always credited on the mandatory end-title "DGA card" along with the assistant directors. Some line producers are credited as both a producer and a UPM; more complex films may even have both a line producer and a UPM. For convenience in this book, we will refer to both of these positions simply as the UPM.

Picking Home Base

If the show is being shot **on location** (that is, not on a **sound stage** or studio **back lot** but in a real place), the show's headquarters, called **home base**, must be selected well in advance. Early on, a **location manager** (who may be supplied by the local film commission) will examine the script and begin surveying possible locations. Local film commissions have extensive files with pictures of various places in their area that are available as film locations; some even publish catalogs or make pictures available on the Internet. The location manager selects from these existing photos and takes new ones as needed, and sends them to the producer, director, and UPM. From these, areas are chosen for further exploration. Weeks before formal Prep is to start, the UPM, the producer, and the director, if available, travel to these areas to survey the possibilities.

Once a suitable area in which to shoot has been selected, the UPM selects the company's home base within that area. Here, the production office, set and costume shops, sound stage (if any), and long-term housing will be located; this will be the nucleus from which the company will venture out to other locations. Sometimes a company will move to other, temporary home bases for portions of the shoot, and each of these becomes a new nucleus for another cluster of locations.

A good location can provide enormous value by saving on construction and dressing costs and can inspire the creative work of the director, the actors, and the production designer. The best locations, alas, are not always logistically or economically feasible: as Sydney Pollack says, "location scouting starts with the creative and ends with the practical—the terrible compromise that characterizes filmmaking."[1]

As Prep begins, the UPM opens the production office at home base with a minimum staff to set up phones, rent office furniture and machines, make local arrangements for housing, set up the accounting office and bank accounts, and generally get ready to conduct business. A week or so later, the rest of the team begins to arrive, and the Prep gets fully under way.

Putting a film company on location is very much like mounting a military operation, and Prep is a busy time: crews are hired, and sets, set dressing, costumes, props, and equipment are planned, constructed, and procured. The actors are called in (or production staff travels to them) for costume measurements and, if needed, wig or makeup preparations. The actors may also be sent any special material that they need to prepare their roles. The HBO film *A Lesson Before Dying*, for example, required a Cajun dialect; I hired a *dialect supervisor*, who prepared a manual and tape recording to be studied by the actors in the weeks prior to the Shoot. With this advance study, and with the assistance and monitoring of a team of dialect coaches, the cast achieved a consistent, believable, and understandable Cajun dialect that contributed greatly to the film's sense of reality.

The Shooting Script

Once the script has been approved in its final form, it must be rendered as a **shooting script** by the first assistant director (**First AD**) with the consultation of the director, the UPM, and the producer. This carefully prepared script divides the show into scenes (numbered consecutively), each of which utilizes a single location (see Fig. 6.1).

The length of a scene is measured in eighths of a page, so Scene 66 in this example would be listed as $1\frac{7}{8}$ of a page. This length is used to estimate how much time will be required to shoot the scene.

The First AD or script supervisor will prepare an estimated **timing** of the script, scene-by-scene, which provides a sense of the show's possible running time. Generally, one full page of standard-format script, like those in Figure 6.1, yields approximately 1 minute of finished program time, depending on the director's style of shooting. The estimated timing may reveal the need for cutting if the show seems long.

It is useful at this point to divide the story into **days**, indicating how time passes, thus determining required changes in costume, makeup, and so on. I like to publish a *time line*, which looks like this:

DAY 1: Scenes 1–5. Late August, 1948.
DAY 2: Scenes 5–7. A week later.
DAY 3: Scene 8. January, 1949.

66 INT. TUSKEGEE HOSPITAL - BRODUS' OFFICE - DAY - 1942   66

Miss Evers stands before him and Douglas. Her face is set.

> MISS EVERS
> They must have penicillin.

> DOUGLAS
> I'm afraid we can't allow that.

> MISS EVERS
> Why not? How long do those men have to
> wait? First in line, that's what you
> said... what you told me. That was the
> promise. Now, there's a drug--

> BRODUS
> Penicillin can't undo the damage that's
> been done.

> MISS EVERS
> It could keep them from getting worse.

> DOUGLAS
> It could also kill them.

> MISS EVERS
> Penicillin?

> DOUGLAS
> (nods)
> Some chronic syphilitics have a fatal
> allergic reaction to penicillin... called
> the Herxheimer reaction. It's been proved.
> Washington is researching the question, to
> determine the degree of risk.

> MISS EVERS
> But they're giving it all over the state.   *
> Caleb Humphries got it, he's fine. He's in
> the goddamned Army!

She puts her hand to her mouth, aghast at the language she
used.

> MISS EVERS
> (continuing)
> Excuse my language.

> DOUGLAS
> Caleb was lucky. Yes, penicillin is   *
> effective, in the primary and secondary   *
> stages.   *
> (more)

CONTINUED

FIGURE 6.1 Pages from a shooting script. Scene 66, *Miss Evers' Boys,* by Walter Bernstein.

CONTINUED:

                    DOUGLAS (cont'd)
        But for those who have entered the   *
        tertiary stage, like the men in our study, *
        it cannot cure, and it may kill! No, for   *
        them, the study has to go to end point.   *

                    BRODUS
        We already have ten years of data--

                    DOUGLAS
        Ten years is not end point.

                    MISS EVERS
        Then what is?

                    DOUGLAS
        Autopsy. Our facts have to be validated by
        autopsy. That is the end point, Nurse
        Evers - autopsy. That will make it
        science, not guesswork.

                    MISS EVERS
                (aghast)   *
        We have to wait until they die?

                    DOUGLAS
        Regrettable, but necessary. Science is   *
        sometimes a hard taskmaster, Nurse Evers   *
        Do you think I like not treating them?   *
        But we must complete the Study! We have a   *
        chance here to make <u>history</u>!

                    MISS EVERS
                (exploding, in tears)
        History is people!   *

        She rushes from the room. Douglas looks to Brodus   *

                    BRODUS
        Let me talk to her.   *

        Brodus goes after Nurse Evers.   *

FIGURE 6.1 Continued

And so on. If the director, the DP, the production designer, wardrobe, make-up and hair, and other key personnel are in agreement in advance on the specifics of the time line, it can greatly enhance the efficiency of the shoot.

As early as possible, the shooting script is sent out by the producer for a **research report**. A research report will check the name of every person and place that is referred to in the script. It will consider whether, in the locale where the story is set, there are any real persons or places that might object to their names being used. If so, the report will suggest "cleared" names (known to be available for use) that can be substituted. All facts and any quotations in the script will also be checked for accuracy. The Art department is meanwhile doing its own research, clearing signage, props, and other visual elements that may have legal implications. All this documented research is critical for the procurement of **E & O** (Errors and Omissions) insurance, which, as we have said, will protect the financing entity against possible lawsuits.

The Board, DOOD, and One-liner

Once the researched shooting script is completed, the First AD, in consultation with the UPM, summarizes each scene in the shooting script on a colored **strip** of cardboard. Each strip indicates whether the scene is day or night, interior or exterior, and it lists the cast members and extras involved and any special requirements, such as rain, props, or vehicles. For quick reference, the strips are in four different colors: white for day interiors, yellow for day exteriors, blue for night interiors, and green for night exteriors. The completed strips are slipped into a rack called the **board**. Nowadays, of course, this is done by computer, although some still prefer the old-fashioned method (see Fig. 6.2).

The development of the board is an ongoing process that requires a great deal of ingenuity and trial and error. The strips are rearranged again and again until the most effective shooting sequence is found. The primary consideration in this process is keeping all the scenes in any one location together in a block. This minimizes the costly **company moves** that take precious time, even if done overnight. For this reason, all the scenes in a given location will be shot before the company leaves that location and moves to another, regardless of the sequence in which those scenes appear in the script. Another important factor influencing the board is the grouping of scenes into blocks that will make viable days or nights of work; film crews usually work 12 to 13 hours a day during shooting, sometimes 6 days a week, especially in television.

Most shows have a number of night scenes, which are usually blocked together; when the company changes over from a day to a night schedule, the First AD and UPM give special thought to how best to "work into" a night schedule gradually, or how to use the longer weekend turnaround to best advantage. Night shooting, by the way, necessitates much more time for lighting and so is more costly.

The board is constantly being adjusted to reflect a host of other considerations, such as the availability of locations and actors; the logistics of travel; the availability of **cover sets** to be used in case bad weather makes

	**--- END OF DAY 13 -- Mon, Oct 21, 1996 -- 3 4/8 pgs.**
5	5	INT	TUSKEGEE HOSPITAL - WARD -'32 *EUNICE IS CALLED TO BRODUS' OFFICE*	DAY	5/8 pgs.	1, 12
0	64	INT	TUSKEGEE HOSPITAL - WARD -'42/45 *PENICILLIN!!*	DAY	1 pgs.	1, 3
67	71	INT	TUSKEGEE HOSPITAL - WARD -'42/45 *BEN'S DYING.......*	DAY	2 pgs.	1, 7, 12
	**--- END OF DAY 14 -- Tue, Oct 22, 1996 -- 3 5/8 pgs.**
33	34	INT	TUSKEGEE HOSPITAL - BRODUS' OFFICE -'32 *THE FUNDING IS DISCONTINUED, EUNICE IS LET GO*	DAY	2 4/8 pgs.	1, 3, 4
71	75	INT	TUSKEGEE HOSPITAL - WARD -'42/45 *SHE SNEAKS IN TO GET THE PENICILLIN*	NIGHT	4/8 pgs.	1, 12
77	81	INT	TUSKEGEE HOSPITAL - WARD -'42/45 *"I KILLED HIM."*	NIGHT	1/8 pgs.	1, 3, 5
3	3	INT	TUSKEGEE HOSPITAL - WARD -'32 *BRODUS SAVES PATIENT'S LIFE*	NIGHT	2 5/8 pgs.	1, 3
	**--- END OF DAY 15 -- Wed, Oct 23, 1996 -- 5 6/8 pgs.**
8A	10	INT	TUSKEGEE HOSPITAL - LOCKER ROOM -'32 *"IT'S GOING TO BE A GREAT THING"*	DAY	7/8 pgs.	1, 12
9	9	INT	TUSKEGEE HOSPITAL - BRODUS' OFFICE -'32 *THEY DISCUSS THE SYPHILIS PROGRAM*	DAY	4/8 pgs.	1, 3, 4
51	50	INT	TUSKEGEE HOSPITAL - BRODUS' OFFICE -'32 *SPINAL TAP? BACK SHOTS!*	DAY	1 2/8 pgs.	1, 3, 4
53	52,54,56PT	INT	TUSKEGEE HOSPITAL - CLINIC -'32 *WILLIE GETS HIS "TAP"*	DAY	2 4/8 pgs.	1, 4, 6
	**--- END OF DAY 16 -- Thu, Oct 24, 1996 -- 5 1/8 pgs.**
5A	6	INT	TUSKEGEE HOSPITAL - BRODUS' OFFICE *"I WANT YOU TO GO MEET SOMEBODY"*	DAY	4/8 pgs.	1, 3
62	66	INT	TUSKEGEE HOSPITAL - BRODUS' OFFICE -'42/45 *"PENICILLIN!" "NO! IT COULD KILL 'EM!"*	DAY	2 1/8 pgs.	1, 3
76	80	EXT	TUSKEGEE HOSPITAL -'42/45 *AMBULANCE ARRIVES WITH HODMAN*	NIGHT	1/8 pgs.	1, 5
78	82	INT	TUSKEGEE HOSPITAL - MORGUE -'42/45 *"YOU KNOW WHAT YOU DID?" "I'D DO IT AGAIN!"*	DAY	1 2/8 pgs.	1, 3, 5
80	84PT	INT	TUSKEGEE HOSPITAL - CLINIC -'42/45 *DR.DOUGLAS HAS SEEN RUBY BLUE!!*	DAY	1 1/8 pgs.	1, 4, 6
81	84PT	INT	TUSKEGEE HOSPITAL - HALL & STAIRS -'42/45 *WILLIE TRIES THE THE STAIRS STEP*	DAY	2/8 pgs.	6
	**--- END OF DAY 17 -- Fri, Oct 25, 1996 -- 5 3/8 pgs.**
	**SATURDAY & SUNDAY OCTOBER 26 & 27 - COMPANY IDLE**
38	40	I/E	GOVERNMENT CAR -'32 *"FIRST TIME IN WASHINGTON?"*	DAY	2/8 pgs.	3, 4
39	41	EXT	FEDERAL BUILDING -'32 *CAR PULLS UP, THEY GET OUT & WALK IN*	DAY	2/8 pgs.	3, 4
	42	INT	FEDERAL BUILDING - STAIRCASE - 33 *MONEY DRIED UP - "COOL DRINK?"*	DAY	6/8 pgs.	3, 4, 13, 14, 15
37B	43	INT	FEDERAL BUILDING - STAIRCASE - 33 *HIPPOCRATIC OATH v. FUNDING*	DAY	7/8 pgs.	3, 4

FIGURE 6.2   A page from a board. Note Scene 66 on Day 17, *Miss Evers' Boys.* **This and other documents from** *Miss Evers' Boys* **reproduced here were created by line producer Derek Kavanagh and First AD James Griffith.**

outdoor shooting impossible; time needed for extensive makeup, hair, or costume preparations; and the available hours of daylight (which may change as the shoot progresses). As planning continues during the weeks of Prep, changes are continuously being made on the board and usually continue to be made throughout the Shoot.

Near the end of Prep, when the preliminary board has been approved, the First AD produces from the board a "day out of days" (**DOOD**), which lists each cast member and indicates the days and dates he or she will start work (SW), work (W), be *on hold* (H) and finish working (FW) (see Fig. 6.3). This document is called a "day out of days" because it shows the number of days each actor works and the total period of time each of them is needed. The DOOD may reveal the need for further changes in the board to consolidate the work period of certain actors. A separate DOOD is also prepared for vehicles, animals, special effects, and other elements of the production.

The last major document prepared by the First AD in Prep is the **shooting schedule**. This contains complete details of everything needed from each department to complete the work planned for each day, scene by scene. This complete schedule is also published in a simplified form called the one-line shooting schedule, or **one-liner** (see Fig. 6.4).

Organizing a film shoot is like building a complex "house of cards" in which every change affects the whole arrangement and can have enormous financial impact. As a result of all these economic and logistic considerations, the scenes in a film are almost always shot out of chronologic sequence, even to the extent that emotionally climactic scenes may sometimes be shot before the scenes that prepare for those climaxes. This puts very special demands on the actors. They must have a strong understanding of the progression and emotional arc of their roles and how each shot and scene will fit into the emotional and psychological progression of their character throughout the entire film.

Final Casting

In the final weeks before shooting starts, the casting of the *supporting players* begins. Some of these roles can be quite large and the actors can work many days if not weeks. A number of **day players**, who work only 1 or 2 days, are hired as well. For all these roles, the *casting director* sends a **breakdown**, a brief description of each available part, to the agents in the area. The agents examine the breakdown and submit photos and resumes of their clients who seem appropriate for each role. The casting director reviews these and decides which actors should be called in for a preliminary, or **screening**, audition. After the casting director has screened eight or so actors, three or four finalists will be given a **callback** to audition for the producer and director.

October	7	8	9	10	11	12	13	14	15	16	17	18	19	20	21	22	23	24	25	26	27	28	29	30	31	1	Travel	Rehearsal	Work	Hold	Holiday	Loop	Stay	Finish	TOTAL
Day Of Month	7	8	9	10	11	12	13	14	15	16	17	18	19	20	21	22	23	24	25	26	27	28	29	30	31	1									
Day Of Week	M	Tu	W	Th	F	Sa	Su	M	Tu	W	Th	F	Sa	Su	M	Tu	W	Th	F	Sa	Su	M	Tu	W	Th	F									
Shooting Days	1	2	3	4	5	6		7	8	9	10	11	12		13	14	15	16	17	18		19	20	21	22	23									
1. Miss Evers	S	W	W	W	W	W		W	W	W	W	W	W		W	W	W	W	W	W		H	W	W	W	WF			22	1			10/7	11/1	23
2. Caleb	S	W	W	W	W	W		W	H	W	W	W	WF																11	1			10/7	10/19	12
3. Dr Brodus												S	W		W	W	W	W	W	W		W	H	WF					10	1			10/18	10/30	11
4. Dr Douglas												S	W		H	H	W	W	W	W		W	H	WF					8	3			10/18	10/30	11
5. Hodman								W	H	W	H	W	W		H	H	W	H	W	W		H	H	W	W	WF			11	8			10/4	11/1	19
6. Willie								W	H	W	W	W	W		H	W	H	W	W	W		H	H	W	W	WF			12	7			10/1	11/1	19
7. Ben								W	H	W	H	W	W		H	H	H	H	H	H		H	H	W	W	WF			8	11			10/1	11/1	19
8. Mr Evers	S	W	WF																										3				10/7	10/9	3
9. 1st Senator																							SWF						1				10/29	10/29	1
10. 2nd Senator																							SWF						1				10/29	10/29	1
11. 3rd Senator																							SWF						1				10/29	10/29	1
12. Betty Parsons													SWF																1				10/21	10/21	1
13. Dr Larkin																SWF													1				10/28	10/28	1
14. Dr Davis																SWF													1				10/28	10/28	1
15. Dr Hamilton																SWF													1				10/28	10/28	1
16. Old Man #1										SWF																			1				10/14	10/16	1
17. Announcer				SWF																									1				10/10	10/11	1
18. Nurse - Sc. 68					SWF																								1				10/17	10/17	1
19. PATIENT #1 - Sc A20												SWF																	1				10/19	10/19	1
20. PATIENT #2 - Sc A20												SWF																	1				10/19	10/19	1

FIGURE 6.3   A DOOD. From *Miss Evers' Boys.*

MISS EVERS' BOYS

Shooting Schedule

Fri, Oct 4, 1996

SHOOT DAY #16 -- Thu, Oct 24, 1996

Scene #6	INT - TUSKEGEE HOSPITAL - BRODUS' OFFICE -'32 - DAY	4/8 Pgs.
	"I WANT YOU TO GO MEET SOMEBODY"	

Cast Members	Props	
1. Miss Evers	keys	**Set Dressing**
3. Dr. Brodus		Large county map W/ pins
		Practical sink.

Scene #34	INT - TUSKEGEE HOSPITAL - BRODUS' OFFICE -'32 - DAY	1 2/8 Pgs.
	THE FUNDING IS DISCONTINUED.	

Cast Members
1. Miss Evers
3. Dr. Brodus
4. Dr. Douglas

Set Dressing
Practical sink.

Scene #66	INT - TUSKEGEE HOSPITAL - BRODUS' OFFICE -'42/45 - DAY	1 7/8 Pgs.
	"PENICILLIN!" "NO! IT COULD KILL 'EM!"	

Cast Members
1. Miss Evers
3. Dr. Brodus
4. Dr. Douglas

Set Dressing
Practical sink.

Scene #50	INT - TUSKEGEE HOSPITAL - CLINIC -'32 - DAY	1 2/8 Pgs.
	SPINAL TAP? BACK SHOTS!	

Cast Members
1. Miss Evers
3. Dr. Brodus
4. Dr. Douglas

Extras
2 other doctors
5 other nurses

END OF DAY #16 - 4 7/8 Total Pages

SHOOT DAY #17 -- Fri, Oct 25, 1996

FIGURE 6.4 A page from a one-liner. For *Miss Evers' Boys*, Scene 66.

If the show is shooting outside Los Angeles, a *local casting director* is hired to cast the day players in that area. This person does initial screening in their area, and three to six finalists are selected for each role. Their auditions are put on videotape and are sent for review by the director, producer, and creative executive. Some directors are willing to cast directly from these tapes, but most often callbacks will be held later, when the director and producer arrive on location. All studios and networks require approval of stars and principal supporting actors, and some even want to approve the day players as well; usually, however, the director and producer are entrusted to cast these smaller parts.

The Last Weeks of Prep

As the first day of shooting approaches, more and more people, equipment, and supplies arrive, and the schedule grows more hectic. Here are some examples of what goes on during these final weeks:

- The final location scout is held as soon as the director arrives on location; the locations are selected and the location manager secures the necessary location agreements and filming permits, and arranges for police and, if necessary, fire protection.
- The art department designs sets and set pieces as needed for the locations selected; set dressing is being accumulated; the props are being assembled.
- If set construction is required, the scene shop works to complete the first sets needed for shooting. Construction crews are sent to the first locations to prepare them. Cover sets (those needed in case of rain) must also be readied for possible use.
- The wardrobe department assembles the costumes, most of them rented, and readies for the final fittings with the actors.
- The camera and lighting equipment to be rented is determined by the Director of Photography (**DP**), the **gaffer**, and the **key grip** in consultation with the UPM. The rental package prices are negotiated, and the camera, grip, and lighting trucks are loaded. The generator that provides reliable power on location is tested.
- The full camera crew arrives and begins checking and testing equipment and film stock; some camera tests are shot to determine which filters and exposure may be used to achieve the **look** desired by the DP and the director.
- The key makeup and hair people arrive, set up their trailer, and begin discussing the actors' makeup and hair needs.
- The principal actors begin to arrive; if the budget has permitted rehearsals before shooting begins, these are held. Costume fittings, makeup, and hair work are completed. Any necessary coaching, musical, or dance rehearsals are held.
- Camera tests of the principal actors' makeup and hair and testing each of their "looks" are done in time to submit them to the network or studio for approval.

The Technical Scout

In the week before shooting begins, the **technical scout**, sometimes called the **reccie** (reconnaissance), is conducted under the supervision of the UPM and the First AD. This is perhaps the most important single event of the Prep; the thoroughness and accuracy of the technical scout will determine the efficiency of the entire shoot.

At a minimum, the scouting party comprises the producer, the UPM/ line producer, the director, the First and Second ADs, the DP, the gaffer, the key grip, the production designer, the set decorator, the prop master, the transportation coordinator and captain, and the location manager and assistant. When possible, it may be useful to include the production sound mixer (more on all of these people in the next chapter). This large group usually travels by bus.

When the scouting party arrives at a location, the director describes in some detail the shooting to be done there. Each crew chief then confers with his or her department to determine the equipment that will be needed and its placement. The locations people and ADs decide where food will be served, snack tables set up, extras housed, and so on. The production sound mixer considers the acoustic environment and warns about airplane, train, and traffic noise; flight paths and train schedules will have been checked, and the locations people will provide for any necessary traffic control during shooting. "Transpo," the ADs, and the Locations department jointly decide where the trucks will be parked so that they will not have to be moved during shooting. The production designer and his or her people discuss the details of set and dressing, and try to get the director to specify the camera's field of vision in each scene to avoid unnecessary work and expense. When all this has been accomplished at one location, the group moves on to the next. This process takes at least 2 days to complete.

In the last week of Prep, when all the various deals have been made and a more accurate estimate of costs is available, the UPM issues a **final budget**, which must actually be signed by the UPM, the producer, the director, and the production executive for the network or studio. From this point on, money is tracked closely; daily **hot cost reports** are issued, which highlight significant variations from the approved budget, and more accurate weekly **cost reports** are also issued by the **production accountant** and the UPM, which show the amount spent to date, the amount needed to complete, and overages and savings for each account in the budget.

The Production Meeting

The last major event of Prep is the **production meeting**. There may be as many as 40 people in the room as the First AD calls the meeting to order: All key personnel and their assistants are present, as are "the suits"—the creative and production executives from the studio or network. The most recent versions of the shooting script, the board, the DOOD, the shooting and one-line schedules, the contact lists for crew and cast, and other essential documents are distributed to everyone.

Each person then introduces himself/herself and identifies his/her job. The producer, the director, and the executives may say some brief words of encouragement and expectation. The First AD then leads the group through the script, scene by scene, describing the main features and requirements of each. It is expected that any lingering questions about what will be needed from each department in each scene will be raised and answered at this time. If the producer, UPM, and First AD have done a good job of keeping all departments up-to-date and in good communication with one another, and if the director has been sufficiently clear on the technical scout, the production meeting need be only a few hours long.

Once the meeting is over, it is expected that the shoot will proceed without a hitch even if changes are made (as they always are).

Summary

Single-camera films are shot piecemeal, and each scene or portion of a scene is rehearsed, staged, and shot at one time, although seldom in chronologic sequence. The production of all films is divided into three periods: the preparation, or **Prep**, the **Shoot** itself, and the period of post-production, or **Post**. Of these, the Shoot is the shortest and costliest but most determines the quality of the finished product.

The line producer and/or UPM is responsible for the budget; he or she is involved with every department and everyone in the production company. One of the first choices to be made is where to shoot. In an effort to reduce cost, many productions have "run away" to Canada.

The company's home base is the nucleus of its operations, from which it may venture out to other locations. Once the final script is approved, it is sent out for research and a preliminary timing of the show is done. The First AD prepares a shooting script that divides the show into consecutively numbered scenes, each in a single location. The needs of each scene are summarized on a colored strip of paper held in a rack called the board. The strips are rearranged to create the most effective shooting sequence, and the proposed sequence generates a "day out of days" that shows when each cast member will work. Finally, the First AD issues a shooting schedule with complete details of everything needed to complete work on each day, plus a short version called the one-liner.

The casting of the supporting and day players is completed, and the remaining crew is hired. With the various deals complete, the UPM issues a final budget. From here on, daily and weekly cost reports are issued by the UPM and the production accountant.

In the last week of Prep, the technical scout is held; at each location, the director describes the shooting to be done there, and each crew chief confers with his or her department. The last major event of Prep is the production meeting.

NOTES

1. Sydney Pollack, in *The Movie Business Book*, ed. Jason E. Squire, Fireside (New York, 1992), p. 50.

CHAPTER

7 The Shooting Crew

When you visit a movie set during shooting, your first impression may be of a lot of people standing around doing nothing. If you watch long enough, however, you will see all those people leap into action when it is time to move the camera to a new position or to move to a new set. If you watch even longer, into the night after the actors have gone home, or early in the morning before they arrive, you will see even more people working very hard to ready the sets, dressing, props, lights, camera equipment, and everything else needed for filming. Make no mistake; shooting a movie is terrifically hard work that lasts 12 or more hours a day, often 6 days a week, for weeks and months without a break. Skill, stamina, patience, an even temper, respect for others, and love for the work itself are necessary. Every person on a set is indispensable at some time or other, and the quality and efficiency of the work depends on each one doing his or her job well.

The Producer

By the time shooting starts, the producer may well have been working on the project for years. In the preceding year, he or she has been involved heavily in the development of the script, and for the past several months has been working full-time to organize the production, making sure that the best available people are hired, and creating an environment and an infrastructure that make it possible for everyone to do his or her best work. On the set, the producer can contribute to a sense of creative enthusiasm and mutual respect by getting to know everyone and making each one feel welcome and valued. However, if the producer has done his or her work well before shooting starts, there will be little else to do during the shoot itself. As producer David Puttnam says:

> Once a film starts, producing is, for the most part, crisis management; you have no other real function. In most respects you're in the way![1]

Given the long-term commitment of the producer to the project, considerable restraint and ego control are necessary for the producer to surrender active control to the director when production begins—but surrender he or she must. The relationship between the producer and the director is the most important relationship on a film set; a lack of trust and mutual respect between them will generate tension that will radiate throughout the company, while a spirit of collaboration will energize everyone.

During the shoot, the producer may or may not choose to be on the set continuously. Many come and go, joining the company only occasionally, perhaps at the start and end of each day's work and during meals. In truth, many directors do not enjoy having the producer looking over their shoulders; however, I usually watch most scenes as they are shot, sitting respectfully behind the director at the video-assist monitor. Being an energetic, "hands on" sort, I have to restrain myself from joining in, but the best role of the producer during the shoot is a reactive one.

The Director

There is much argument about whether or not the director is the primary creator (as in "auteur") of a film. Writers may feel one way about it, producers another, and studio or network executives yet another. But all will agree that once production starts, the director must be the primary authority on all creative questions. A director friend of mine once admitted that "Ninety percent of directing is being willing to accept the responsibility." Filmmaking is complex, and a film company involves many disparate talents and skills; without a clear central authority, it would quickly dissolve into anarchy. This is not to say that the director is a bully (though some are) nor that he or she tries to control every detail of the film (though some do). Many directors invite and respect the collaboration of everyone on the team, leading by example and maintaining a quiet authority.

Besides being a central authority, the director is the "central intelligence" that translates the words of the script into the total sensory experience of the film. Although a good screenwriter has written with a strong visual sense, his or her words must nevertheless be rendered as actual people and places. In this, the director instructs and aligns the work of the actors, the DP, the production designer, the editor, the composer, and everyone else to produce a unified result in which the whole is greater than the sum of its parts.

There are as many directorial styles as there are directors, ranging from the total improvisation of John Cassavettes to the detailed, shot-by-shot planning of Alfred Hitchcock. Most producers, if given the choice, would prefer Hitchcock's way of working. As Pollack himself admits, "Every time the director says, 'Let's *try* it this way,' instead of 'Let's *do* it this way,' money is being spent at enormous rates."[2] If the director's plans are known in advance, it is far easier to budget and schedule efficiently. Although, few directors will go as far as Hitchcock (a former art director) did and actually prepare a **storyboard** showing the planned composition of each shot, some will at least supply a **shot list** for the day's work, listing the intended shots for each scene. Such a list helps the DP, the gaffer, the set dressers, and everyone else to prepare one or more shots ahead to minimize the time it takes to move from one scene to another. A shot list also helps the First AD to pick the best times for breaks, and lets the producer know how far along the company is within the body of the day's work. In the absence of a shot list, the producer may, as the sun is setting, be reduced to asking, "How many shots will there be in this last scene?" The answer he or she least wants to hear is "We'll find out when we get there," though it is often the truth.

During actual shooting, the director controls the staging of the scene, the interpretation and business of the actors, any adjustments to the script (within limits), the physical world of the scene (set, dressing, costumes, props, makeup, and hair), and the camera shot and lighting. Only the director may call "action" to start a shot and "cut" to end it, determine which takes are printed, and say when it is time to move on to another shot. In post-production, the director will continue to exercise creative control, up to a point; few directors get **final cut**, and eventually the film will probably pass to the control of the studio or network, when it can be recut, remixed, and even reshot. But during Prep, Shoot, and most of Post, the director is the captain of the ship.

The **second unit** director, if any, is in charge of a small unit (often around 30 people) that shoots peripheral material that may or may not involve principal actors. Smaller units of only a few people, called **splinter** or **second camera units**, may be broken off from the main company to shoot simple material like **establishing shots**, often without sound (or as a German director might say, "mit out sound," hence, **MOS**).

The **editor** begins work as Prep ends, and the editorial department is set up and ready to receive the first dailies as shooting starts. The relationship of director and editor, both during the shoot and after, is especially important and is discussed in Chapter 10.

The Assistant Directors and Script Supervisor

As discussed, the First AD, along with the UPM, is mainly responsible for organizing the shoot, and his or her organizational skills can make the difference between staying on schedule and budget or not. But the ADs do much more.

During shooting, the First AD functions as a sort of "first officer," speaking with the authority of the director in handling the logistics of the shoot; this leaves the director free to concentrate on creative matters. For instance, the First AD makes sure the necessary preparations are being made for each shot so the company moves smoothly through the schedule. He or she conducts the actual business of shooting. In addition, he or she is responsible for calling meal breaks during the day and sets the call times necessary to give each actor and crew member adequate time off.

The Second AD supports the work of the First AD by arranging the **background** in each scene, such as extras, vehicles, animals, and so on, and he or she may exercise some creativity in staging these elements. The Second AD also prepares **call sheets** and **production reports** which list the day's activity, such as the number of camera setups, scenes completed, amount of film consumed, and so on.

There is usually a Second Second AD who works away from the camera, generally at **base camp** (where all the trailers are parked), making sure the actors and everything else needed will be ready on time. This person handles most of the personnel paperwork such as call sheets, extras' vouchers, W2s, I9s, and union forms. There will also be *Set PAs* (production assistants) doing anything else that needs doing. You can easily spot any of these people; they all wear walkie-talkies.

Another team member who works very closely with the director and editor is the **script supervisor**. These unsung heroes are responsible for **continuity**, making sure that it will be possible to cut from take to take with everything matching: the words, the actors' positions, the amount of water in the glass, which words were spoken when the actor drank, *everything* down to the smallest detail. This is no small feat, especially when hours and even days may elapse between one take and another in a given scene. The script supervisor records the specifics of every shot on his or her script for the guidance of the editor (more about this later). He or she also notes which takes are to be printed and the total pages shot each day, and he or she provides the timing of each scene as shot, which is compared with the original estimate and is useful in determining if the show is running long or short. The script supervisor may even advise the director about **eye-lines** and whether further coverage is needed for a scene (more on this later).

The Camera Department

The director of photography or cinematographer (**DP**) is usually the highest-paid person below-the-line, and with good reason, because only the director has more influence over the quality of the film and the efficiency of the shoot. The DP, in consultation with the director and production designer, will determine **the look** of the picture, which is controlled by lighting, filters, exposure, and choice of film stock. He or she also determines the position, the frame, and the movement of the camera (again with the consultation of the director).

In England, the DP is called "the lighting cameraman," and as that term indicates, control of the lighting is the most crucial element in the DP's artistry.

The DP heads a large department. First is the camera crew, which comprises the **camera operator** and two assistants, the First and Second AC (assistant camerapersons.) A few DPs prefer to operate their own cameras, although special permission must be received from the union for this; when two cameras are run simultaneously to save time, a second or *B Camera* operator is needed, although some DPs operate the B camera themselves if the union permits. The First AC or **focus puller** sets the focus by measuring the distance from actor to lens (see Fig. 7.1) then maintains the focus throughout the shot and is also responsible for changing lenses and filters, setting the lens aperture and shutter angle per the DPs instructions, and **checking the gate** after each shot to make sure no film emulsion or other dirt has ruined the take. The Second AC or *clapper/loader* lays down the marks that the actors must stand on during the scene, loads and unloads the film magazines, keeps track of the amount of film stock used and other camera department paperwork, and operates the clapstick and board that provide the **slate** at the start of each take. When two cameras are being run simultaneously, there may be a separate loader just to handle the large amount of film used.

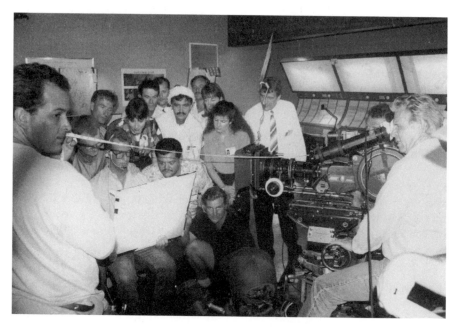

FIGURE 7.1   **A camera crew at work. Note the tape that the focus puller is using to measure the distance between the actors and the lens.**

On most shooting days, the greatest amount of time is spent on lighting, which makes the **gaffer** a very important person. He or she works for the DP to execute the lighting and is assisted by a **best boy** (or **best girl**) who heads the crew of **electrics** (electricians). The electric truck carries their equipment. On location, power is supplied by a **genny** (generator) that is run by its own operator.

When something needs to move, a **grip** does the moving. Named after the little satchel of tools they once carried to work, the grips are headed by the **key grip**. This resourceful group lays **track** and sets up **cranes** for the camera; the **dolly grip** moves the camera dolly as necessary. The most important job of the grips is to modify the lighting by setting the various devices that shape and control the light sources, such as **flags**, **scrims**, "choppers," huge "20 × 20s," and "blacks." They also black out location interiors for night interior scenes and put gelatin color filters on windows for day interiors. If "wild" (moveable) walls on the sets need to be moved, grips move them. There is not much a grip may not do; they are the handypersons of the set and usually have a belt full of tools and tape around their waists.

The Sound Department

The **production sound mixer** is in charge of recording the dialogue and sits near the set at his or her sound cart on which are mounted the various recording devices and the mixing board. The **boom operator** is in charge of the microphones, both the ones suspended above the actors and—when that is impossible—the radio microphones concealed in their clothing. There may also be a third person to handle the cables and, if necessary, to operate a second microphone.

During shooting, the sound mixer listens carefully over headphones to check the clarity of the actors' voices and for any extraneous noises, such as airplanes or traffic. The production sound mixer's most important responsibility is to capture a perfectly clean recording of the dialogue He or she also provides remote radio headsets to the director, the script supervisor, and other people who may need them. In special situations, such as a scene in which the actors are dancing, the sound mixer will supply **playback** of the music or a **click track** giving only the tempo of the music. Playback may sometimes be broadcast to the actors through "earwigs," tiny speakers hidden in their ears like hearing aids.

The Art Department

Everything seen in a film—sets, dressing, costumes, props, and so on—is the responsibility of the **production designer**. He or she will usually collaborate with the director and the DP in creating the "look" of the picture and is responsible for translating the descriptions in the script and the images in the director's mind into a tangible reality.

As head of the art department, the production designer has a number of assistants and controls a large portion (as much as 10%) of any picture's budget. The department is so large that there is often a separate **art department coordinator**. The **art director** is the designer's first assistant and interprets the designer's concepts as drawings, though there is usually an additional *draftsperson*. The detailed drawings for the construction department are prepared by the **construction coordinator**, who supervises the carpenters and painters who build and finish the sets.

On the set, the **set decorator** "dresses" the set to create a believably complete world and is responsible for his or her department's budget. The set decorator and the *lead person* procure and manage the set dressing, which is installed and struck by a **swing gang**. If there are plants, flowers, sod or trees involved, indoors or out, they are handled by a **greens person**.

The **prop master** has the special responsibility of providing and managing everything the actors handle (as distinct from the set dressing) and controls the prop budget. He or she has to consider not only the realism of the props, but also the way in which they are used and the personality of the characters who use them. Actors often form strong emotional attachments to personal props, such as glasses and rings because they come to embody aspects of the character. A good prop master will understand and encourage this and will provide several choices of personal props for the actor and director. Some actors may want to use or wear bits of their own props or clothing to help "anchor" their performance, as did an ancient Greek actor who had an urn containing his son's real ashes brought to him on stage. If firearms are used, the prop master will be in charge of safety considerations.

The **costume designer** collaborates with the production designer but is also a creative force in her or his own right. Costumes have a special power in creating the world of a film, especially in "period" stories. Regardless of the period, costumes also express the personalities of the characters; a good actor will feel the psychological support of a well-chosen costume and, as with props, may form a special attachment with a favorite sweater or hat. The costume designer considers the temperament of the character and the actor and also the historical, economic, and social aspects of the story, the season, the overall "palette" of the picture, and the changing look of the character as the story progresses.

The costume designer's right-hand person is the **wardrobe supervisor**, who makes and controls the wardrobe budget. She or he oversees the execution of any constructed costumes by the *cutter*, the *seamstress*, or the costume house. During shooting, the wardrobe supervisor and crew make sure each actor has the right clothing for each scene in plenty of time to dress, and they maintain and clean the costumes throughout the shoot.

Around the Actors

The people with whom the actors tend to spend the most time and are often most intimate are the **key makeup person** and the **hair stylist**. Stars will usually require their own makeup and hair people. In any case, the choice of these people will be based not only on their artistic ability, but on their social skills as well. The time in the makeup trailer is an important preparation time for the actors; it is a refuge for them during that nervous period just before shooting. The atmosphere in the makeup trailer helps determine the atmosphere of the entire set, and the makeup and hair people can be important allies of the producer in helping to ensure an efficient and happy set.

Besides creating a design that enhances each actor's appearance and approach to the role, the hair and makeup people must keep track of each character's look in each scene, especially because they are often shot out of sequence. If there are special makeup needs, such as old age, scars, wounds, or fantastic transformations, the makeup designer is responsible for **prosthetics** (rubber pieces glued to the actor's skin), and the hair stylist handles wigs and hair pieces. Wigs are used not only in period movies, but also when an actor's real hair is inappropriate. In *Miss Evers' Boys*, for example, Alfre Woodard's own hair was quite short, so four wigs were built for her, each with a different look; this saved both hair styling time and wear and tear on the wigs (a good human hair wig can easily cost more than $4000). Crowd scenes make special demands on the makeup and wardrobe departments, and extra assistants are brought in as needed.

Depending on the demands of the script, there may also be a number of coaches who work with the actors, such as the dialect coaches we used in *A Lesson Before Dying*, and general acting coaches, usually called **dialogue coaches**. The **stunt coordinator** sets up any stunts, supervises stunt persons, works with the actors to stage fights or other physical action in which they are involved, and is responsible for their safety.

The *Company Nurse* is available to everyone for first aid and helps ward off colds, headaches, sore backs, and other ailments that must not be allowed to interfere with the Shoot.

Transportation

A large part of every film budget is spent on transportation. The person in charge is the **"transpo" coordinator**, who rents and supervises the maintenance of the vehicles. There is also a transpo *captain*, who does the hiring and firing of the drivers, as well as checking drivers' work hours to conform to regulations of the Department of Transportation. The transpo department makes sure the crew, actors, and equipment trucks are where they need to be and on time.

An important part of the transpo coordinator's job is to procure and maintain the vehicles that are driven on camera, called "action" or "picture" cars, and the background vehicles that dress outdoor sets. This can be especially important (and difficult) in period films. Key vehicles may be "doubled" with one for exterior use and another pre-rigged with lighting and camera mounts for interior driving scenes. When the script calls for driving scenes, a special vehicle called an **insert car** is used. The insert car tows the picture car or sometimes a lowboy **process trailer** on which the picture car may be placed along with lights and camera. We had an exciting day on *Miss Evers' Boys* when an insert car and process trailer inadvertently wandered off the controlled route and into real traffic; it was one of those crises that justify the producer's presence on the set.

One of the most important vehicles on a set is not controlled by transpo; the *catering truck* is a self-contained kitchen. Like an army, a movie company travels on its stomach, and food is important in maintaining morale. The meals served by the caterer are important social occasions that help revive spirits during the long days. In addition to regular meals, a table full of snacks and drinks is maintained continuously near the set by **craft services** to keep everyone's blood sugar and cholesterol levels up.

In the previous chapter, we mentioned the work of the location manager in securing permissions for locations, as well as making all local arrangements for police and fire support. During the shoot, the location department provides everyone with maps and directions to the various locations, places directional signs on the route, arranges for parking, and deals with any unexpected problems with the local authorities or inhabitants; nothing attracts a curious crowd faster than a movie shoot.

Meanwhile, Back at the Office

Often overlooked, but of crucial importance, is the staff in the production office. In a very large production, the UPM may have the help of a *production supervisor* or an *assistant UPM*. The office staff and its operation is supervised by the **production coordinator**. This important person is the hub of all communications for the company and knows where everyone is and where to get whatever might be needed by anybody. The coordinator distributes critical documents such as contact lists, crew and cast lists, production reports, call sheets, and so on. An *assistant production coordinator* and various *office PAs* work under the coordinator, depending on the size of the company. They handle all conceivable support services from cell phones to laundry.

Of special importance is the **production accountant** who, depending on the size of the production, will have one or more assistants. A mountain of paperwork is funneled through this office, from which all expenditures are carefully recorded and the daily **hot cost** and all-important weekly **cost**

reports that keep each department apprised of their financial condition are generated. The UPM, accountant, and studio or network production executive discuss the cost reports regularly by telephone, sometimes daily if there is a problem.

Summary

Every person on a movie set is indispensable at some time or other. There is little for the producer to do during the shoot except crisis management. The director is the central authority that aligns the efforts of every department toward a unified result. During shooting, only the director may call "action" to start a shot and "cut" to end it. The First AD handles the logistics of the shoot. The Second AD is responsible for the background in each scene. The DP will determine the "look" of the picture and be in charge of the camera crew, which comprises operator, focus puller, clapper loader, and dolly grip. Control of the lighting is a crucial element in the DP's artistry, and the gaffer works to execute it, assisted by a best boy or girl. Grips move things, especially the devices that modify the lighting. The production sound mixer and boom operator record the dialogue.

The production designer is responsible for everything seen in the film, assisted by the art director. The set decorator "dresses" the set. The costume designer, assisted by the wardrobe supervisor, expresses the personalities of the characters through their clothing.

The people with whom the actors tend to spend the most time are the key makeup person and the hair stylist. Besides creating a design that enhances each actor's approach to the role, the hair and makeup people must keep track of the character's look in each scene.

The transpo coordinator rents and supervises the maintenance of vehicles. Back at the production office, the production coordinator supervises the office staff and all communications. The production accountant records all expenditures and generates the all-important cost reports.

NOTES

1. David Puttnam, in *The Movie Business Book*, ed. Jason E. Squire, Fireside (New York, 1992), p. 38.
2. Sydney Pollack, in *The Movie Business Book*, ed. Jason E. Squire, Fireside (New York, 1992), p. 45.

8 Shooting I

Single-Camera

In the previous chapter, you met most of the members of the single-camera production team; now we describe the actual process of shooting. As discussed, there is much waiting between takes for lighting, so much so that single-camera filmmaking could be described the way I once heard a commercial airline pilot describe flying: endless periods of boredom punctuated by moments of sheer terror.

Rehearsal

Even though some film directors insist on having a period of rehearsal with principal cast members before shooting actually starts, such advance rehearsal time is unusual, especially on remote locations. It is very expensive and may necessitate actors being brought to the location days or weeks before they are scheduled to shoot. More often, especially in television, an actor will report to location only 2 days before he or she must actually perform, with costume fittings having been done previously. In most circumstances, rehearsal for each scene occurs on the set just before the scene is lit.

Because lighting and other technical matters take so much time during shooting, the actors can often get together to run lines and feel their way through a scene, sometimes under the supervision of the director, sometimes not. Film actors tend not to rehearse blocking or external movements for fear of developing a mechanical or premeditated quality; they simply review the lines and—for themselves individually—the inner process that lies beneath the lines. The only exceptions are fights or other physical business that could be dangerous, which are carefully rehearsed.

It is always assumed that the actors will arrive on the set with their lines memorized. However, because films are shot in such small pieces, it is usually possible for the actors to do their final memorization on the set. On the day of shooting, half-size copies of the script pages to be shot called **sides** are distributed to everyone.

Calls

Once shooting is under way, each day's work is announced on a **call sheet**. It is distributed at the end of each day and lists the following day's work in shooting sequence, with the calls (the time when people must report to the set) for each department (see Fig. 8.1). Although the intention is to stick to the sequence of work originally planned on the board and shooting schedule, last minute changes must sometimes be made during shooting because of unforeseen things such as illness, unfinished work being carried forward, or bad weather. When this happens, the call sheets indicate the change. If the change affects many days of shooting, a new board and one-liner may be published on a different color paper.

Union regulations require that under most circumstances actors and crew members must have a minimum number of hours off between calls. This time off is called the **turnaround**. It is an important factor in determining the start time for each day's work, depending on when work finished the day before. Actor and crew turnarounds are different, with the crew getting less time off, depending on their union and department. Actors must have at least 12 hours off; this must include transportation time to and from the set (except in Canada). The Screen Actors' Guild (SAG) also requires that actors must give their permission for their turnaround to be broken. In *Miss Evers' Boys*, for instance, Alfre Woodard was in nearly every scene, and I had to ask her to break her turnaround on more than half of the 23 shooting days. (It is a tribute to her professionalism and commitment that she always agreed, although the succession of long days tested her stamina; as it turned out, she won the Emmy, CableAce, Golden Globe, and SAG Awards for her performance.)

During the time of year when daylight hours are short, or when there is a long drive to the location, or when there is extensive makeup and hair work, the actual time a given actor is available for shooting may be greatly reduced. With children, additional time must be set aside for schooling. I once produced a film in which the three stars were a woman with an extensive hairdo, a child, and a dog; there were days when we were lucky to have 8 hours of actual shooting time.

When the total hours worked in a day exceed 8, federal law requires that overtime must be paid at premium rates. The amount of the premium is different for different types of workers. When a union turnaround or required meal time is violated, additional penalties must be paid; any realistic budget includes a considerable allowance for overtime and penalties, because it is cheaper to pay these penalties than to prolong the Shoot.

Each day's shooting begins with the arrival of the ADs, wardrobe, hair and makeup personnel, and the actors who are "up" first that day (some actors may have very early calls because of extensive makeup or hair work). The actors dress and perhaps make an initial visit to the hair and makeup

Miss Evers' Boys	Crew Call: 7:30 AM					Call Sheet
Pahana Productions						
1252 W. Peachtree St. Suite 100						Date: Monday, October 21, 1996
Atlanta, GA 30309	Shooting Call: 8:30 AM					Day 13 of 23
(404) 897-5456						Location: Kirkwood Elem School
fax (404) 897-3545						
Director: Joseph Sargent						Sunrise: 7:47 AM
Executive Producers: Robert Benedetti, Laurence Fishburne						Sunset: 6:57 PM
Producers: Derek Kavanagh, Kip Konwiser						

Scenes	Set	Cast	Pages	D/N	Sequence	Location
3	INT. Hosp -Clinic '32	1 ,3	2 5/8	N2	1932	Kirkwood Elementary School
	Brodus saves patient's life.					701 Kirkwood Dr.
						Atlanta, GA 30307
50	INT. Tusk Hosp Clinic '32	1, 3, 4	1 2/8	D	1932	
	Spinal Tap ! Back Shots					
9	EXT. Tuskegee Hosp '32	1, 3, 4	7/8	D4	1932	
	They discuss the syphillis program					
* *	TIME PERMITTING	* *				
**52, 54	INT. Hosp -Clinic '33	1 ,4 ,6	(2 4/8)	D20	1933	
	Willie gets tapped.					
**56pt.	INT. Hosp -Clinic '33	1 ,6	(1/8)	D20	1933	
	Other patients have left					Nearest Hospital:
						Dekalb Medical Center
						2701 North Decatur Rd.
		Total Pgs:	4 6/8			Decatur, GA 30030
						404-501-1000

Cast - Weekly & Day Players

Character	Cast	Status	Leave	Makeup	Set Call	Remarks
Miss Evers	1. Alfre Woodard	W	6:40 A	7A	8:30 A	P/U @ Grand
Dr. Brodus	3. Joe Morton	W	7:10A	7:30A	8:30 A	P/U @ Grand
Dr. Douglas	4. Craig Sheffer	W	7:40A	8A	8A	P/U @ Grand
Hodman	5. Von Coulter	H				courtesy pick-up @ Grand
Willie	6. Obba Babatunde	W	8:40 A	9A	10A	P/U @ Grand
Ben	7. Thom Gossom, Jr.	H				courtesy pick-up @ Grand

Stand-Ins				Atmosphere	
1 Miss Evers Stand-in			@ 8:30 A	14 patients	7:30 A
1 Douglas stand-in			@ 8:30 A	5 Nurses	7:30 A
1 Brodus stand-in			@ 8:30 A	1 adolescent w/ chest bandage	7:30 A
1 Willie stand-in			@ 8:30 A	3 Doctors	

Advance Shooting Schedule				Special Instructions:	
				Props: antiseptic, bandages, false torso, needle, syringe, stethoscope	
Day 14	TUES. October 2 2				
71	INT. Tuskegee Ward '42/45 N	1, 7	2	Grip & Elec: tent in clinic windows	
75	INT. Tuskegee Ward '42/45 N	1	4/8		
82	INT. Hospital Morgue '42 N	1 ,3 ,5	1 5/8	Makeup: makeup to match fake torso	
80	INT. Tuskegee Hallway '42/45 N	1 ,5	1/8		
DAY 15	WEDNESDAY OCT. 23			Wardrobe: surgical gown & mask	
5	INT. TUSKEGEE WARD '32	1, 12	4/8		
10	INT. " "	1, 12	7/8		
45	INT. " "	1, 12	3 2/8		

** NO FORCED CALLS WITHOUT PRIOR APPROVAL FROM UPM **

Unit Production Manager	1st Assistant Director	2nd Assistant Director
Derek Kavanagh	James Griffin	Jonathan Watson

FIGURE 8.1   **A call sheet**

departments. (The makeup, hair, and wardrobe process is sometimes called **the works**, as in "put the actors through the works," or "she's in the works.")

Perhaps a **rigging crew** has worked on the set the day before (or sometimes through the night) preparing the set and laying cables for the lights. When the main crew arrives, it begins setting up for the first shot; flooring or **track** may be laid so that the camera dolly will move smoothly, lighting equipment is readied, and so on. The actors are soon called to the set to go through the first scene with the director and the DP.

The Line-up

At the camera, the actors usually read through the scene, then walk it through. In this process, called the **line-up**, the director, actors, and DP work out the positioning of the characters in the scene, called the **blocking**. Simultaneously, the director and the DP are designing the camera positions; the blocking of the actors and the camera is done in relation to one another.

As the blocking pattern is set, the Second AC (clapper/loader) sets **marks** on the floor—colored pieces of tape with a different color for each actor; these indicate where each actor's feet are to be at key moments in the scene. As they perform the scene, the actors must "hit their marks" exactly, without looking down; the composition of the shot and the focus of the camera require the actor to be in a precise location at a precise time. It may even matter which foot the actor's weight is on, or how they hold themselves when seated, because the camera's **depth of field** (the range of sharp focus) may be only an inch or two.

Once the marks have been placed, the First AD releases the actors (the **first team**) and sends them back into the works. The First AD then calls for the **second team**. These are the **stand-ins** who repeat the blocking pattern while the DP and the gaffer adjust the lighting. The camera operator and DP also set the exact positioning of the camera, which has its own blocking marked by the dolly grip. At each blocking position, the focus puller measures and notes the distance between the actor and the lens. The three people it takes to run a film camera—operator, focus puller, and dolly grip—must function as a harmonious team during the take.

The lighting and camera preparation for a shot can take hours. Meanwhile, the first team is dressing, rehearsing, or having the final touches put on their hair and makeup. During this time the first team is managed by the Second Second AD, who must be aware of the whereabouts of each actor at all times.

During breaks for lighting, or on days they might otherwise not be working, the actors may be called for one of the necessary PR (public relations) chores that plague movie sets, such as behind-the-scenes interviews or posed "gallery" photos. Even during shooting, there will probably be a **still photographer** at work; these experienced people use special sound-proofed cameras and are expert at blending into the background. More obtrusive are the video crews that appear on the set (on days carefully chosen and negotiated by the producer) to shoot **B-roll** of selected scenes for use in promotional material called the **EPK** (electronic press kit), used on shows such as *Entertainment Tonight*. As bothersome as all this PR activity is, it is an important part of the promotion of the show, and most actors (not all) cooperate willingly.

The Second Second AD gives the actors their advance warnings as the time to report to the camera approaches and makes sure that the necessary wardrobe, makeup, and hair work is done in time. Because scenes are shot out of chronologic sequence, the makeup, hair, and wardrobe people check to see what "script day" a scene is; Polaroid photographs document each character's "look" for that particular day to guarantee continuity. Shooting out of sequence makes it critical that the actors review their parts to know how to start each scene and how the scene should end to best lead into the scene to follow.

When the lighting and camera preparation is finished, the first team is recalled to the set for shooting; they are expected to report promptly, ready for work. The cardinal rule is that although everyone must wait for the camera, *the camera must never wait for anyone.*

Shooting

At the camera, the actors assume their starting position, called **first marks**. The first shot is usually the **master**, the widest and most inclusive view of the scene. Subsequent shots, called **coverage**, are from various camera **angles**. These usually "tighter" shots of one or two actors (called **singles** and **two-shots**) will later be inserted into the master by the editor. The camera's field of vision is called the **shot size**, as in "wide shot," "medium shot," "close up," and "extreme close up" (see Fig. 8.2).

When a shot requires an actor to look at another who is off-camera, his or her eyes must be placed in precisely the right place; if the **eye-lines** of the various characters are not consistent in the various shots of a scene, the scene cannot be cut together. Actors serve one another by standing off camera to provide the correct eye-line, and they play the scene with full intensity. (Not all actors need or want this kind of off-camera support. When Henry Fonda was shooting *On Golden Pond*, he was surprised when his daughter Jane—who played his daughter in the movie—appeared off-camera to provide his eye-line. He told her to go and rest, saying, "It's called acting, dear.")

Each segment of shooting is a **take**. Each take is often preceded by a quick check of costume, makeup, and the distance between the actor and the lens (the focus puller uses a tape measure for this, as illustrated in Figure 7.1). The director and the DP, accompanied by the script supervisor and the producer, gather around a small video monitor behind the camera; this

SIZE OF SHOT

Possibly the most elementary decision that the director makes is the size of shot. At each precise moment of a scene how close is the subject to the lens? How much is included in the frame? How much is left off screen?

It is a decision about 'content'. The director must decide on the meaning of the image at this instant. The point of 'proxemics' theory is that the camera -- as imaginary observer -- has a psychological attitude to the character, a feeling very clearly defined by the distance between the subject and the lens. The closer we (the camera) are to the performer, the greater the 'empathy'. The further away we are the more we are 'objective', disinterested, uninvolved. Increase in shot sizes creates a rise in tension: a decrease relaxes our feelings of participation.

D.W. Griffiths said "the camera can photograph thought." Moreover, it does so in a double sense. At very close quarters, the camera can scrutinise the unspoken and internal feelings of thought that are 'betrayed' by the eyes. But, at the same time, the shot size (as well as the editing) makes a statement about the director's thoughts and feelings about the subject.

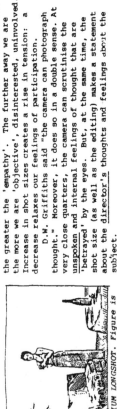

LONGSHOT. Figure is too far away to hear conversation or to see facial expressions.

MEDIUM LONGSHOT. Figure is 'theatrical' scale as on stage. Performance is projected.

MEDIUM SHOT. Hip length. A conversational level of exchange. The literal sense of words balanced with 'non-verbal' meanings.

CLOSE SHOT. Head and chest. More personal. Feelings and thoughts are visible and carry as much weight as the meaning of the dialogue.

CLOSE UP. Head only. More 'interior' feeling. Dialogue may now be less significant than 'subtext'--the things that are not verbalized.

BIG CLOSEUP. Eyes and mouth now 'betray' the things words cannot say. As an image size, it is 'too close for words'.

shows the **video assist** that is fed directly from the camera as the scene is shot. The video assist is usually recorded, and it may be useful at times for the director and DP to review earlier shots. (The clutch of people around the monitor is sometimes called the "video village.") It is expected that everyone except the director, the DP, the script supervisor, and the producer will stay away from the monitor during shooting out of respect for the director's need to concentrate on the scene.

When the company is shooting on a sound stage (rather than on location), the First AD will call "red light" or "**on a bell**," a bell rings (literally or figuratively), and warning lights inside and outside the sound stage light up to stop anyone from entering or leaving. Air conditioning is stopped and everyone stands still and falls utterly silent with no whispering, no matter how far away from the camera. If the shoot is outdoors, the ADs and PAs are stationed at various places to hold traffic and let everyone know that "we're rolling." All these restrictions remain in effect until the director cuts the take and the call of "clear" is sounded.

When everything is ready for the take, the First AD calls "**rolling**" and the production sound mixer starts the recorder. When the recorder is up to speed, the sound mixer calls "**speed**." (In our digital age, this is instantaneous and merely signals that the sound mixer is ready.) The production sound mixer also **slates** the audio tape, as in "Scene 8 baker, take 2." The camera operator starts the camera as the clapper/loader places a **clapper board** (which nowadays has a digital display) in front of the lens to record the numbers of the scene, shot and take, calling out "mark" as he or she hits the clapstick on top of the board (or stops the digital display) to establish the synchronization point for sound and picture.

The take begins when the director calls "**action**" and ends only when he or she calls "**cut**." It is extremely important that the actors do not begin before the call of action, nor stop before the call of cut. Only the director is allowed to control shooting in this way. If an actor forgets lines or misses a mark, he or she may stop performing, but only the director can stop the camera. When the take is interrupted, the director may keep the camera rolling and tell the actors to "pick it up from" some recent point in the scene, or the camera may be stopped and the take restarted. Each time the take is redone, the actors are sent to their opening positions by the First AD (who calls "first

---

FIGURE 8.2   **Shot sizes. This material was written and drawn by the late Alexander Mackendrick, Founding Dean of the School of Film and Video at the California Institute of the Arts. Mr. Mackendrick directed such great films as *The Man in the White Suit*, *The Ladykillers*, and the Academy Award-winning film, *The Sweet Smell of Success*. His book on film grammar and dramatic form will be published by Faber and Faber, London.**

marks" or "back to one"). If it is necessary to redo only a portion of the scene, it is called a **pickup**.

During each take, the production sound mixer, script supervisor, and director listen over headphones to the dialogue being recorded. The microphones are extremely sensitive, and it is unnecessary (and undesirable) for the actors to "project" as they would in a theater. When Ralph Richardson, already an accomplished stage actor, did his first film role, he asked the director after his first take how it had gone. The director, who was sitting behind the camera, said "It was fine, Ralph, except I could *hear* you." Film actors must speak exactly as they would in a real life situation, even to the point of whispering if required by the scene. When time permits, certain off-camera lines may be recorded without picture as **wild lines**.

When the director is satisfied with a take, and the DP, camera operator, and sound mixer concur that it was technically acceptable, the director will tell the script supervisor to **print it**. Work then begins on the next shot, which is a **new deal**.

A scene may require many shots. Figure 8.3 shows the six camera angles required to cover Scene 66 from *Miss Evers' Boys*. The director, Joseph Sargent, blocked the scene so that Nurse Evers was torn between the two doctors, who were on opposite sides of the room for much of the scene. The challenge to Director of Photography Donald M. Morgan was to light the entire room simultaneously while keeping the light sources out of the frame.

Here is a list of the shots used to cover this scene. Each of these six shots needed between two and five takes. (Please reread the scene in Figure 6.1.)

Scene 66: A "flowing master" of the entire scene starting as a two-shot favoring Evers (played by Alfre Woodard) with Dr. Douglas (played by Craig Sheffer) in the background; Douglas comes forward into an over-the-shoulder two-shot favoring him; the camera then follows him across the room into a two-shot with Dr. Brodus (played by Joe Morton); Douglas then returns to the two-shot with Evers to deliver the bad news ("Autopsy"); finally the camera follows him back to his starting position in a medium single for his last lines.

66A: A closer single of Douglas for his final lines of the scene.

66B: A close single of Evers through most of the scene, especially as she hears the bad news through her exit. This is the crucial shot of the scene.

66C: An over-the-shoulder shot looking past Evers to Brodus at his desk; focus shifts (is **racked**) as she turns to face Douglas (who has now returned to his desk behind her); Evers then exits frame and camera ends on Brodus for his last line and exit.

66D: A close single of Brodus for most of the scene; this shot will provide good **cutaways** if they are needed.

66E: A wider single of Brodus for his opening lines.

Shot 66   **Four Positions from the Master**

"They must have penicillin!"

"I'm afraid we can't allow that."

"It's called the Herxheimer reaction."

"Autopsy."

Shot 66A

"We have a chance to make history here."

Shot 66B **Two Positions from the Closeup of Evers**

Her reaction to "autopsy."

Her exit.

(continued)

FIGURE 8.3   Covering a scene. From Scene 66, *Miss Evers' Boys*. Courtesy of *HBO*.

Shot 66C Two Positions from the Racking Shot

"That will make it science, not guess work."   "We have to wait for them to die?"

Shot 66D

"Let me talk to her."

Shot 66E

"Penicillin cannot undo the damage that's been done already."

FIGURE 8.3   Continued

Each time the camera is moved, it is a new **setup**, and the lighting must be adjusted. The whole process continues until all the shots required to complete the scene have been made. The six shots needed for the scene from *Miss Evers' Boys*, for example, took some 6 hours to shoot.

At the end of each shot, the AD calls **"check the gate."** If the gate is clear of any accumulated film emulsion or other dirt that might have ruined the shot, the company **moves on** to the next scene. This process is repeated until the next-to-last shot of the day is reached, called the **Abby Singer** after a legendary producer. The last shot of the day is called the **martini** for obvious reasons. The end of shooting for the day is a **wrap** (as is the end of the entire Shoot). At wrap, the call sheet for the next day's work is distributed, and the First and Second ADs begin to prepare the production report of the days work.

The film shot during the day is organized and inventoried by the loader, then sent to the laboratory by transpo, special courier, or overnight air. At the laboratory, the film is developed, and the takes identified by the director are printed. These **dailies**, usually transferred to videotape, are delivered the next day to the director, the editor, the producers, and the executives. In the first days of shooting, the DP may order a few dailies on film to be sure the look of the show is correct. (The increasing use of high-definition digital video [HD] requires a somewhat different process than the film process described here. This is discussed in Chapter 13.)

Script Changes

Throughout the shoot, script changes may be made by the director and/or the producers to meet the demands of locations, weather, or other exigencies of shooting. Sometimes actors will suggest rewrites of their lines. All significant changes in the approved script must be cleared in advance by the network, the studio, or the other financing entity, and this is an ongoing part of the producer's responsibility.

When changes are made, new script pages containing the changes are issued. These changed pages are different colors, with the sequence of colors established by tradition (blue, then pink, yellow, green, and so on). On each new page, the changed lines are marked with an asterisk in the margin (notice the changed lines in Figure 6.1). By the time the show has been shot, many colors of paper will have been used, and the completed script is called a **rainbow script**.

Lines are sometimes altered slightly by actors as a scene is shot, either to personalize them, or to make them more comfortable in the mouth, or simply because film actors learn their lines more "loosely" than do stage actors. The high degree of spontaneity and authenticity required by the camera encourages the film actor to "rediscover" his or her lines each time the scene is shot. Some film actors say they like to "learn the action, not the words." Here, for example, is a speech from *Miss Evers' Boys* as written:

> Some chronic syphilitics have a fatal allergic reaction to penicillin . . . called the Herxheimer reaction. It's been proved. Washington is researching the question, to determine the degree of risk.

Here is the same speech as delivered by the actor, with the changes indicated:

> Some chronic syphilitics *suffer* a fatal allergic reaction to penicillin . . . *It's* called the Herxheimer reaction. *Now*, it's been *proven*. Washington is *doing a study right now* to determine the degree of risk.

The latitude given to the actors to make such changes varies, depending on the attitude of the director, producers, and network or studio. Again, the producer and director must decide on the spot whether a change is within acceptable limits or not. (Much to their chagrin, writers are rarely present during shooting, except in episodic television and sitcoms, where the writers are often also the producers. The WGA is currently fighting for the presence of writers at cast readings and on the set.)

Assuming that slight changes are allowed, they are recorded by the script supervisor during the first take. It is necessary that in subsequent takes the words match the first to allow for editing, and the script supervisor will correct the actors if they go astray. The script supervisor records each shot and each printed take on his or her script (called the **lined script**) with special markings and notations. These pages are sent along with the dailies to the editor and are invaluable in guiding him or her in assembling the **rough cut** of each scene (see Fig. 8.4). (The editor and other post-production personnel and processes are examined in Chapter 10.)

Summary

The work to be done each day is announced the day before on the call sheet. Rehearsal for each scene usually occurs on the set just before the scene is lit. In the line-up, the director works out the blocking, which is recorded by marks on the floor, while the DP sets the camera angles. Once the scene is blocked, the First AD releases the actors and calls for the "second team," who stand in while the DP adjusts the lighting and the camera positioning. The first team is then recalled to the set for shooting. The cardinal rule is that though everyone must wait for the camera, the camera must never wait for anyone.

The first shot is usually the master, the widest and most inclusive view of the scene. Subsequent coverage is from various tighter angles. When a shot necessitates that an actor looks at another who is off-camera, his or her eyes must be on precisely the right eye-lines.

Each segment of shooting is a take. The director, the DP, the script supervisor, and the producer gather around a monitor that shows the video assist. The First AD calls "rolling," and the production sound mixer starts the recorder and calls "speed." The camera operator rolls the camera as the

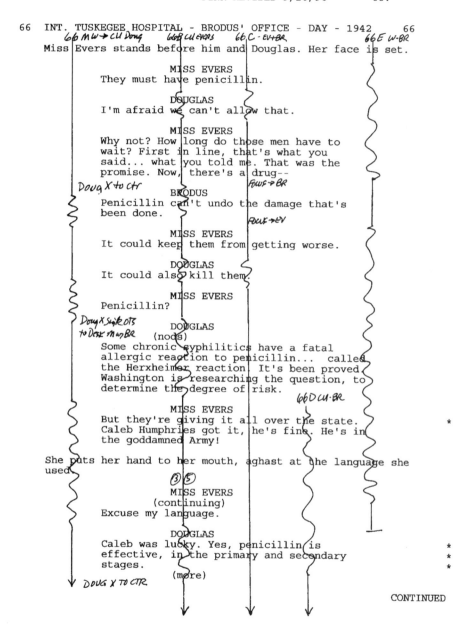

FIGURE 8.4   A script supervisor's lined script. Each take is marked by a line indicating where it started and ended, with notes describing each. A squiggly line indicates that the line is spoken off camera.

Second AC slates the scene with a clapper board. The take begins when the director calls "action" and ends only when he or she calls "cut."

A scene may require many shots. Each time the camera is moved, it is a new setup, and the lighting must be adjusted. The process continues until all the shots required to complete the scene have been made, when the company moves on to the next scene. After the day's work has been wrapped, the film is sent to a laboratory and developed. The takes identified by the director are transferred to videotape, and the dailies are delivered the next day to the director, the editor, the producer, and the executives.

When script changes are made, new pages are issued in different colors. Changes made during shooting are recorded by the scripting supervisor, who also records each shot on his or her lined script. These pages are sent along with the dailies to the editor to guide him or her in assembling the rough cut of each scene.

CHAPTER

9

Shooting II

Multiple Cameras

We have described the process for shooting single-camera film. We turn now to the multiple or so-called three-camera format. The unique aspect of this format is that several cameras run simultaneously during an entire scene, and the entire output from each camera is recorded. In this way, a scene can be captured in its entirety far better than with a single camera, although the lighting needs to be more general, and the camera angles must be more restricted, than in single-camera film. Sitcoms ("situation comedies") and soap operas are always shot in the three-camera format. These may be shot in either film or video, but in either case the simultaneous use of multiple cameras radically changes the production process.

The three-camera format was originally designed to produce angles similar to the basic two-shots in single-camera film, as Figure 9.1 shows. The center camera is getting the master, while the two side cameras have the side angles, called **complementary** because they are of equal size, making it easy to cut from one to the other. In recent years, the number of cameras has been increased to four to provide greater flexibility in shooting, although we still refer to this as a "three-camera" setup.

Multiple-camera shooting has evolved over the years, and today the four cameras are not at all restricted to the basic shots described in Figure 9.1. The director plans shots in advance, and each camera is given a **shot list**; while one camera is getting the shot planned by the director at a particular moment, the others are setting up for the subsequent shots, so that a considerable variety of angles and shot sizes can be achieved. The cameras are constantly adjusting for new shots; this requires tremendous skill from the teams operating the cameras. In the hands of a seasoned director with a top-notch crew, the four-camera setup can produce a surprising variety of angles and sizes, sometimes approaching the range of single-camera shooting.

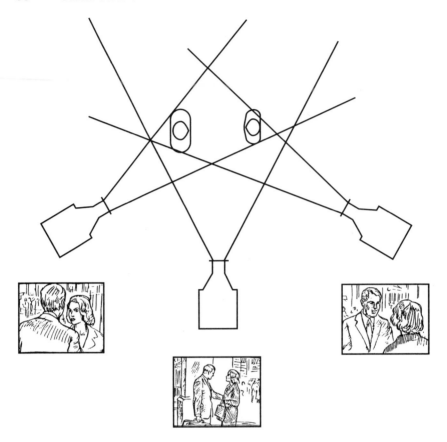

FIGURE 9.1   **The three-camera layout. Drawings by Alexander Mackendrick.**

Film Versus Video

Soap operas must be produced as quickly as possible because they air 5 days a week. This means that there is no time to process film, and so soap operas are shot in video. Sitcoms, on the other hand, air only once a week and are usually shot in film. Film and video are under the jurisdictions of different unions with different work rules and pay scales. There are also mechanical differences: Video cameras are operated by a single person who does all the moving and focusing, with the help of a *cable puller*, who manages the umbilical cord that connects the camera to the control board and recorders. Film cameras, however, even for sitcoms, need the usual three-person crew of operator, focus puller, and dolly grip. Watching four three-person camera crews performing an intricate ballet as they shoot a sitcom can be as much fun as watching the show itself.

Despite the greater cost of shooting in film, the fact that sitcoms are often dubbed into other languages and sold in foreign markets make the use of film cost-effective. If they were shot in video, the transfer from video to film that would eventually be required would be very expensive, at least at the current state of telecine technology.

There are also important differences in the shooting process between soap operas and sitcoms. In video soap operas, where editing time is extremely limited, the director switches from shot to shot "on the fly" (as the scene is performed); only limited changes may later be made. The director sits in a control booth and calls the shots ("ready two, take two") while the **technical director** does the actual switching. The director is talking constantly to the camera operators to set up and adjust their shots. If the director has to speak to the actors, he or she does so over an intercom, or through the floor manager.

In film sitcoms, the director need not call shots and is on the floor with the actors and cameras. He or she is watching what the cameras see via a video assist from each camera displayed on a "quad" monitor (the screen split into four quadrants) and may adjust shots by speaking directly to the camera operators. In general, however, the sitcom director usually pays more attention to the actors' performances than to the cameras and trusts each camera operator to report if they made their assigned shots or not. Meanwhile, a technical director is in a separate booth switching the video assist coming from each film camera from shot to shot; this provides the "edited" show watched on monitors by the live audience during the **taping** (although sitcoms are now shot on film, the final performance is still referred to as the "taping").

Sitcoms

Ever since Desi Arnaz got the idea of bringing a live audience into the tapings of *I Love Lucy*, a live audience has become essential to the energy and "presence" of sitcoms. The broad, sometimes farcical comedic style required for a sitcom flourishes when the actors receive the rush of adrenaline that only a live audience can provide. Moreover, the timing required for good comic delivery, with the setup and payoff of "three jokes to the page," can be perfected best when the actors are getting the reactions of a live audience.

The rehearsal and shooting process of a sitcom, with only one half-hour show shot per week, is very similar to live theater. Having 4 or 5 days of rehearsal allows the actors and the writers to develop the material and the performance in a way that would be impossible in soap operas or in single-camera film. Here, for example, is a typical week on a show like *Frasier:* work on each episode begins on a Wednesday and culminates with the taping the following Tuesday night.

Wednesday: The cast meets for a few hours to sit at a large table and read the script (this is the **table reading**). At the reading and at all subsequent rehearsals, the director, the producers, and the writers provide exuberant laughter; this sometimes seems artificial to an outsider, but it is essential to the actors in developing their comedic timing.

Executive producers of sitcoms are usually also the head writers. These people are called "show runners" and they create and shape the continuing life of the show, providing story and character continuity and developmental arcs for the characters. Additional writers are brought in to work on specific episodes; in all, the average number of writers on each episode is approximately six.

After the reading, the director and the actors share their ideas with the writers, and, after some discussion, the writers cloister themselves in "the room" to work on improvements. The room is strictly off limits to anyone but the writers, and they sometimes work through the night to prepare the script for the next day. In fact, the week long rehearsal period for a sitcom is more for the sake of developing the material than it is for preparing the actors and camera crews, who could probably shoot an episode in 2 days if they had to.

Thursday: Again, a table reading is held to test the improvements in the script. After more discussion of the script, the show is put into the set for basic blocking and the development of comic business and "sight gags."

The "standing" or "home" set is familiar to the actors; each character has established their territory and habitual traffic pattern, so the blocking is more or less automatic. The entire set is laid out as a very wide proscenium set might be arranged in the theater. It is much wider than it will look on camera. The extra width permits the bulky film cameras to move more easily and to get more oblique angles, which provide better shot composition (see Fig. 9.2).

To allow quicker changes from set to set, sitcom home sets contain more than one room; the *Frasier* set, for example, includes Frasier's living room, the kitchen, and the radio booth. These rooms are side by side, with the adjoining walls swinging so that parts of the set may be opened or closed as needed. If any given episode requires additional sets, they are placed at one end of the stage or the other.

Friday: Final blocking and more rehearsal on the set. The actors get their marks, just as in single-camera film. Positioning is important, because two or more shots from different angles may depend on the actor's placement, but the cameras can adjust slightly if an actor is not exactly on the mark.

At this rehearsal, props, special set dressing, and wardrobe are introduced. The director and the DP are planning the shots. The most recent script improvements from the writers are distributed, and the actors are beginning to commit their lines to memory.

FIGURE 9.2   **A sitcom being shot. Notice the four cameras and the extra width of the set. Photo courtesy of** *Frasier*, **Paramount Studios.**

The Weekend: The writers are probably working over the weekend to improve the script further. Each cast member has a fax machine at home to receive any new pages. If necessary, other writers may be brought in to "punch up" the script; these are specialists, sometimes called "body and fender people," who have a knack for recognizing incipient jokes and bringing them into focus.

Occasionally, an outdoor scene, or a scene requiring some sort of special effect, may be shot separately during the week and inserted into the show at the taping.

Monday: Camera blocking is done today as the full crew reports for the first time (some of these crews work on other shows on other days). The actors may have to assimilate improvements made by the writers over the weekend, and they finally begin to learn their lines in earnest. This is usually a critical day in the development of the show, and energy is high.

Tuesday: Dress rehearsal is held in the afternoon with an invited audience. The large number of background extras are worked into the show by the Second AD. Many of these extras have been with the show for some time, and the whole affair has the atmosphere of a party. The dress rehearsal is filmed, and on rare occasions, material from it may be used in the broadcast version. After the dress rehearsal, a dinner is served to cast and crew (the principals have a quiet private dinner of their own) as the audience begins to arrive. Improvements from the writers are coming in until the last minute, even between the dress rehearsal and the performance. At "half hour," the actors report to wardrobe, hair, and makeup.

The taping at 7 P.M. that evening has the feeling of an opening night in the theater. A live band is playing, and a "warm-up person," a stand-up comedian with considerable familiarity with the show, keeps the audience entertained both before and during breaks in the taping. The audience sits in bleachers across the entire width of the sound stage, so not everyone can see the action when it is on one of the side sets, and most of the time the bulky film cameras make it difficult to see the actors anyway. It matters little, though, because video monitors are hung above the audience so everyone can watch a rough version of the show, switched from shot to shot. This is important because the audience's reactions are recorded and serve as the "laugh track" for the show. If an outdoor scene has been pre-shot, it will be inserted into the show at the proper point so that the audience's reaction to it can be recorded as well.

As the taping begins, the cast is introduced to the studio audience with much applause. Energy is way up. The floor in front of the set is filled with people: the director, producers, writers, agents, studio and network executives; when an actor looks toward the audience, they see a virtual mob of people and cameras watching them. During performance, this crowd is in constant motion and presents a real test of the actor's concentration (see Fig. 9.3).

A bell signals the beginning of each take. If during the taping a mistake is made (which is common), the director stops and restarts as necessary, usually picking up from some point; often, a scene may be entirely redone.

When a scene is successfully completed, the actors retreat for any necessary costume changes while the sets and cameras are moved into place for the next scene. The warm-up person keeps the audience occupied; the great fear, of course, is that the spectators will grow tired during the 4 or more hours it will take to tape the show, and their reactions may fall off toward the end. (When necessary, laughter may be "sweetened" by mixing various tracks or even by electronic augmentation.)

To avoid exhausting the audience, many of the shots that need to be redone are saved and done as pickups after the audience has gone home. These pickups may go on for hours; lines may even be rewritten at this point, and I once saw an entirely new ending for an episode of *Cheers* written and shot at 2 o'clock in the morning.

FIGURE 9.3   **What a sitcom actor sees. Beside the four cameras, there is a host of producers, writers, network and studio executives; the audience can be seen in the bleachers in the background. Photo courtesy of *Frasier*, Paramount Studios.**

The next day (Wednesday), the process begins all over again with a table reading of the script for the next episode. Meanwhile, the show just shot is being edited and mixed. Most sitcoms work 3 consecutive weeks, then take a week off, producing 24 or 26 shows a season.

Soap Operas

"Soaps" and sitcoms have some similarities with live theater and with each other: in both, scenes are shot in sequence and in their entirety, stopping and restarting only as necessary; also, the actors in both perform continuously because they are always potentially on camera. But there the similarities end.

Because "soaps" air every weekday, there is little time for rehearsal, or to do much stopping and starting during the taping. At the end of each day, the scripts for the next day's shooting are distributed, and the actors must learn their lines overnight. The next morning, rewrites may be handed out, sometimes just before a scene is shot. The camera blocking is roughed in, and most of it is done "on the fly" by the director talking to the camera operators over their headsets. Despite this improvisational atmosphere, there is great pressure to complete every scene in one take. You can see why soap opera actors and crews must be able to think on their feet.

Summary

There are two kinds of shows commonly shot in the so-called three-camera format: sitcoms and soap operas. Nowadays, four cameras run simultaneously so that the performance can be captured in its entirety. Because of time constraints, soap operas are shot in video, while sitcoms are usually shot in film. Video cameras are operated by a single person who does all the moving and focusing, while film cameras always require a three-person crew.

There are ways in which three-camera shows are closer to live theater than to single-camera film. First, scenes in three-camera are played through in their entirety and in sequence. Second, the actors must perform continuously because they might be on camera at any time. Third, a live audience has become essential to the energy and "presence" of sitcom performances. Only one half-hour episode is shot per week, and 5 days of rehearsal allow the material and performance to be developed in a way that would be impossible in soap operas or in single-camera film.

Because "soaps" air every weekday, there is little time for rehearsal or to do much stopping and starting during the taping; the actors and crew must be able to think on their feet.

CHAPTER

10 Post I

Editing

Three-camera shows need only the most rudimentary post-production; sit-coms are edited and mixed in a single week, and soap operas are aired virtually as shot. Single-camera films, however, must undergo a much more extensive post-production process. In fact, single-camera film as shot is like the larval stage of a butterfly; it will reveal its true beauty only when it has spent considerable time in the cocoon of post-production.

During post-production, the *editing* process fulfills the flow, shape, and pace of the story; the addition of **effects** enhances realism and excitement; the addition of *music* enhances the mood and punctuates important moments; any problems in the dialogue are fixed; and the **timing** (adjusting the color and brightness) of the print and video transfers completes the intended look of the picture. The common phrase, "we'll fix it in Post," is truer than you might imagine.

The post-production period is longer than the Prep and Shoot combined—anywhere from 5 weeks for a 1-hour network episodic drama, to 12 to 16 weeks for a small television picture, to 42 weeks or more for a feature film. Post is divided into three periods: roughly one third for editing the picture, another third to add music and effects, and the final third for **dubbing** and **printing**. The weekly cost of Post, however, is much lower than the Shoot; where the production unit employed 100 or more people full-time, Post requires as few as four to eight people at any one time. The money and time spent on Post is handsomely repaid in enhanced quality, and it is a shame when delivery dates sometimes cause the Post to be rushed.

When shooting ends, the line producer/UPM turns over the day-to-day control of the project to the **post-production supervisor** (in television called the "co-producer" or "associate producer") who works closely with the network or studio's post-production executive, who now joins the team to make final approvals on the major steps of post-production.

The Editing System

At the end of Prep, just as shooting started, the editing system was installed and readied to receive dailies so that the editor could begin to assemble scenes as they arrived.

There are a very few editors, such as Michael Kahn and Anne Coates, who still edit (**cut**) film by hand, using a **Movieola** or **flatbed** editing machine, surrounded by strips of film hanging from racks, the tails falling into piles held by canvas bags. Some very great films, such as Steven Spielberg's *Saving Private Ryan*, have been cut this "old-fashioned" way. The vast majority of films, however, are now edited on so-called non-linear computerized systems, primarily the **Avid**, which is driven by a Macintosh computer and operated with an ordinary computer mouse.

In a computerized system, the dailies are transferred to videotape and arrive at the editing room with the film, sound, and video information encoded in a *telecine transfer log*, commonly called the **flex file**. Just as scene numbers are the main reference points during shooting, **time codes** are the main reference points during post-production; they enable everyone to identify and access specific frames and sequences anywhere in the film. There are three main kinds of codes: The first is the *audio time code*, which is generated by the production sound mixer on the set and encoded on his or her sound tapes (this is often simply the time of day when the scene was shot). The second is the *video time code*, which is generated when the dailies are transferred from film to videotape in **telecine**; the video time code shows hour, minutes, seconds, and video frame numbers (30 per second), appearing as 1:00:00:00. Each cassette of dailies has its own time code running consecutively throughout the cassette, with the first cassette starting at hour 1, the second cassette starting at hour 2, and so on. The third kind of information in the flex file is the *key code* listing the frame numbers printed on the edge of the film stock itself. These three pieces of information may be displayed according to the editor's preference in **windows** on the daily itself (see Fig. 10.1).

When the dailies are loaded into the editing machine, they are **digitized** and stored in memory along with the information in the flex file. The shots comprising each scene become a *gallery* of thumbnail pictures; any shot or take can be accessed instantly by clicking on it and can then be manipulated and inserted into the film assembly.

The assistant editor keeps track of all these details. The Editor's Guild defines the assistant editor's job as simply "to be of assistance to the editor," and this can mean many things: he or she supervises maintenance of the equipment, provides additional material like stock footage and temporary music and effects, lays in temporary titles and cards, renders some of the choices made by the editor, and does any number of other tasks.

FIGURE 10.1   A daily with windows. Shown are the audio time code (*upper left*), video time code (*lower left*), and film key code (*lower right*). The actor is Joe Morton in *Miss Evers' Boys*.

The Editing Process

As soon as dailies are delivered from the set, the editor begins to assemble scenes as they are shot. A good editor is usually able to keep up with the Shoot. This is extremely important, because if there are problems the editor can alert the director in time for additional shooting. For example, during the Shoot of *Miss Evers' Boys*, Mike Brown, our editor, informed director Joe Sargent that he needed more crowd reactions to use as **cutaways** in several dance numbers; his warning came before the dance set had been struck, so we were able to squeeze in a hasty trip back to the location, reassemble the extras, and shoot the necessary additional footage, incurring only modest overtime costs.

The editor owes his or her first allegiance to the director. In fact, many directors have a team consisting of a First AD, a DP, and an editor with whom they work regularly. The producer is wise to respect the director's wishes in hiring these people, because the enhanced communication and cooperation among them is invaluable. (Producers and executives, by the way, should avoid interposing themselves between the director and any of his or her key collaborators; the relationship between director and actors is especially sacrosanct.)

During the Shoot, the director and the DP probably had a good idea of how each scene might eventually be edited, and this idea guided them in their choice of angles and coverage. Some directors even "edit in the camera," meaning that they shoot only the material needed to assemble the scene in the way they intend. Creative executives are often on the lookout for this, and the producer will frequently get a call demanding that he or she ask the director to "give us more coverage!" There are some studio and network executives, in fact, who pride themselves on recutting the films delivered by directors. This is why directors will sometimes try to protect their work by *camera cutting*.

On the other extreme are the directors who cover everything; in episodic television especially, some directors shoot "everything that moves," giving the editor and producers a lot of choices. A director's **shooting ratio** (the ratio of film shot to film actually used) is a cost consideration; a low-budget indie director may have to keep the ratio around 1:3; in other circumstances, a director may shoot around 1:12, some even more. I once acted on an episode of *LA Law* in which the director shot enough film to make an average MOW.

Once all the printed takes from a scene are installed in the editing system, the editor chooses the takes to be used—an actor's performance can actually be improved by careful shot selection. The editor must also decide which angles to use and exactly when to cut from one shot to another. A good editor finds a motivation for each cut: it may come from a movement of an actor's eyes or from the need to see a reaction to something that has happened (in film, *reactions* are always more interesting than *actions*). Good cutting will also fulfill the rhythm of the scene. In all, a good editor's choices are rooted in *storytelling*. This is why, of everyone who works on films, editors most often become successful directors.

There are a number of editing choices available for making the transition from shot to shot. The most common is the simple cut; this is fairly neutral in its effect. Special emphasis or a mood can be obtained by such transitions as a **smash cut** (an unexpectedly extreme change in perspective) or a **lap dissolve** (meaning that one image overlaps another as the first image fades and another appears). Dissolves are of various lengths; for example, a fast dissolve, also called a **soft cut**, lasts only four to eight frames; because film runs at 24 frames per second, a soft cut lasts one sixth to one third of a second. A medium dissolve might last 24 frames (1 second), and a long dissolve might last 96 frames (4 seconds) or more.

The end of a sequence or section of action might be signaled by **fading to black**, followed by a **fade in** of a new section. **Whiteouts** (a dissolve to white) often imply a loss of consciousness. Certain styles of filmmaking call for old-fashioned devices such as **wiping** from one scene to another. Other editing devices are **freeze frames** (simply printing the same frame over and over), jerky fast-motion or stutter cuts (eliminating some frames), and **slow-mo** (slow motion, achieved by doubling or tripling every frame; of course, the shot may have been photographed in slow motion by increasing the speed of the camera, called **over-cranking** from the days when film cameras were literally cranked by the operator).

There is a surprising number of things that can be done during editing to alter what was shot. The composition of a shot, for example, can be altered to some degree by **blowing up** (enlarging) and repositioning it; a shot may also be **flipped** (reversed) if there is no writing visible in it, and even run backwards. When the negative is eventually cut, these altered frames are specially developed and inserted as **opticals**, along with the other opticals such as dissolves, superimposed titles, and cards. Opticals are expensive, which may be a consideration for independently financed pictures.

The Director's Cut

By the time the Shoot is wrapped, the editor has nearly finished assembling much of the picture. The Editor's Guild mandates a period of time, depending on the type of project, for the editor to finish his or her *first assembly*, also called the *editor's cut*, which, by DGA rule, is shown *only* to the director. (There are several versions of a film, each called a **cut**.) DGA rules then give the director a period of time (currently 3 weeks for television films and 6 for features) in which to refine the film to produce the *director's cut*; during this period, no one except the director, editor, and assistant editor are allowed to see the film unless invited to do so by the director.

In an effort to provide an accurate sense of the director's intention for the finished picture, **temp (temporary) music** and even some **temp sound effects** such as thunder, traffic noise, or night crickets will be added to the director's cut; this material is usually provided by the assistant editor. Temp music is culled from CDs, and temp sound effects are pulled from sound effects records. Some dialogue changes, and off-camera lines may even be inserted at this point via a microphone. An Avid system has a number of audio tracks as well as modest mixing capabilities, so surprisingly good temp mixes can be achieved. I have seen some pieces of temp music and effects actually re-mixed into the final picture.

The director's cut is first delivered to the producer, who may suggest some changes, which the director may or may not incorporate; the *producer's cut* is then delivered to the network or studio. The network or studio then gives its notes, which are discussed with the director and producer; the results of this discussion are executed by the editor. This process can last for weeks or months, with various versions of the film bouncing back and forth between the network or studio and director. The struggle between directors and their studios over control of the **final cut** has sometimes been epic in scope, and the contractual right to control the final cut is the most sought-after prize among directors. Without this guarantee, even famous directors are likely to lose in a dispute with the network or studio. For example, Sir Richard Attenborough was forced to deliver his film *Chaplin* at a certain length, and felt that the 7 or 8 minutes he was forced to cut greatly harmed the film. Likewise, Terry Gilliam waged a public war over Universal's decision to cut the last 11 minutes of *Brazil*, a deletion that radically altered the meaning of the film, but which the studio argued was necessary to shorten the film and permit three showings per night in theaters.

Previews, Focus Groups, and Re-shoots

If there is a disagreement about a major editing decision (such as exactly how to end the film) the studio or network may decide to *preview* ("test screen") the film to measure the audience response. Producer David Puttnam describes this:

> Previews are immensely valuable. It's the first time you learn how your preconceptions fit with those of the actual audience . . . There are two types of preview: for production and for distribution. The production preview points up the strengths and weaknesses of the movie and allows us to make improvements before the final mix.[1]

As a result of a preview, or even without one, it may sometimes be decided to **re-shoot** some material, even to the point of altering the storyline. Large-scale re-shoots are costly because they are essentially mini-productions requiring the start-up of an office and the hiring of new personnel, the recreation of some sets, and the retrieval of costumes, props, and dressing (it is common practice for certain costumes, props, and dressing to be held in reserve until the editing process is completed in case a re-shoot is ordered). In *Miss Evers' Boys*, for example, we decided to re-shoot all the scenes in the Senate hearing room and the final cemetery scene. The show was originally shot in Atlanta, but this 2-day re-shoot was done in Los Angeles weeks after the show had wrapped, and it cost over $250,000. Because of improvements in set, lighting, casting, and some rewriting, the re-shot material greatly improved the film.

Re-shoots are not always so extensive. Sometimes it is discovered that a simple **insert**, such as a character's point-of-view (**POV**) of a prop, can help explain something that puzzled the preview audience or can provide a cutaway that hides a gap left by deleted material. As Puttnam points out:

> I've always tried to leave some money in the budget for re-shooting a couple of days of odds and ends, useful inserts learned about in previews. This 'shooting to the cut' is remarkably economical (with an almost 1:1 shooting ratio) and can solve enormous problems.[2]

Many studios, networks, and cable companies use what Puttnam calls the "distribution" preview as standard procedure; it is often called a **focus group** and is used to help determine the most effective marketing campaign. There are market research companies that specialize in conducting focus groups: A sample audience is assembled and shown the film with temp music and effects; after the showing, the audience is given a questionnaire to complete, and a brief discussion is held; the results are then interpreted and quantified. Network studio executives place great importance on these results, often trusting them more than their own artistic judgement.

Eventually, the editing process is completed, and the cut is **locked**, meaning that no further editing can be done. At this point, an entirely new phase of post-production begins.

Summary

During Post, the editing process fulfills the flow, shape, and pace of the story; the addition of effects enhances the realism and excitement; the addition of music enhances the mood and punctuates the action; problems in the dialogue are fixed; and the timing of the print and transfers complete the intended look of the picture.

The post-production period is longer than the Prep and Shoot combined. Post is divided into three periods: roughly one third for editing, another third to add music and effects, and the final third for dubbing and printing. Most films are now edited on computer-driven systems. The film is transferred to video dailies, then digitized along with a flex file that correlates audio and video time codes and the film key code. A good editor can usually keep up with the Shoot and can alert the director if there are problems in time for additional shooting.

The editor decides which shot to use at any given moment, and exactly when to cut from one shot to another to best shape the scene. A good editor's choices are always rooted in storytelling. After wrap, the editor completes the editor's cut; DGA rules then give the director a period of time to produce the director's cut, which may contain temp music and effects. Studio or network notes are worked through. There have been epic battles between directors and studios over control of the final cut. The film may be previewed, resulting in a re-shoot of some material or simply providing feedback for marketing.

Eventually, the editing process is completed, and the cut is locked, meaning that no further editing may be done.

NOTES

1. David Puttnam, in *The Movie Business Book*, ed. Jason E. Squire, Fireside (New York, 1992), p. 39.
2. Ibid.

11 Post II

Sound

As soon as the cut is locked, work begins to prepare the original negative for printing; this painstaking and time-consuming process will continue for several weeks, as discussed at the start of the next chapter. While the negative is being prepared, work begins in earnest on the sound track for the film; this cannot be done until the cut is locked, because all sound must be synchronized to picture. In this phase of Post, a number of sound elements—dialogue, effects, and music—are prepared, then blended together in a **final mix**. Although the post-production supervisor and editor (along with the producer and director) remain actively involved, the **supervising sound editor** now assumes leadership of many aspects of the project.

Spotting and Sound Design

The first major step in the sound editing process is **spotting**, a session at which the director "spots" the exact placement of sound effects (a separate spotting session is held for music, which is discussed later). At the sound effects spotting session, the director's overall ideas about sound are discussed: Should the sound effects be minimal, realistically complete, or stylized? The locked cut is then run, and the desired effect in each scene is discussed; should the environment of the scene seem busy or serene? Do we want to keep the outside world alive or create a sense of isolation? The director indicates exactly where major sound effects are to be placed; these are used to create mood or to punctuate the action. As Sydney Pollack says,

> It's possible radically to alter what an audience feels by tiny variations from literal reality in the sound track: when a sound starts and when it fades; whether it cuts off or overlaps slightly into the next scene . . . The sound track can guide the audience often as much as the visual.[1]

From this session, the sound editor begins to form ideas about an overall sound design, and a spotting list is prepared with the specific frame references for each cue. The sound editor then begins to assemble the necessary sound materials that will be needed during the final mix. He or she considers not only the demands of realism, but also mood, environment, the need to fill voids in the production track, and ways to enhance transitions. A number of elements are collected in a "library" of sounds, for which individual cues will be created. Most sound designs consist of many *layers* of sound elements. A TV movie may use hundreds of tracks, a big feature may use a thousand.

Looping

One of the first things the supervising sound editor does is to review the **production track**, the tapes made during the Shoot. He or she must decide what bits of dialogue will need to be replaced by the process called **looping**, also called Automatic Dialogue Replacement (**ADR**). There are many reasons why dialogue from the production track may need to be replaced: poor sound quality, background noise, or a poor line reading by the actor are the most common. The sound editor prepares lists of cues to be replaced (see Fig. 11.1), and the necessary actors are called in (the actors' contracts include required looping days).

The ADR supervisor is in charge of the looping stage. The portion of the scene to be corrected is projected on a large screen while the actor listens to the original production track over headphones. If the section of dialogue to be replaced is longer than a phrase, it will have been broken into short pieces by the sound editor. As the portion of dialogue to be replaced approaches, the actor hears three warning beeps over the headphones; on what would be the fourth beep, the actor speaks, synchronizing his or her voice to match the picture, with whatever improvements or adjustments may be required.

Several takes are usually necessary to achieve a final result that marries seamlessly with the production track. Looping is a skill that can be quickly learned by most actors. The legendary producer John Houseman once told me that Sir John Gielgud, called to loop a very long speech in Shakespeare's *Julius Caesar*, waved away the little pieces of dialogue prepared by the looping supervisor and read the entire speech in one take, synchronizing perfectly to every frame of the film.

ADR may also be used to replace lines that have been rewritten to improve the story or to account for material that has been edited out. These changed lines must be written to fit the existing mouth movements; this is not a problem in a wide shot, but it can be tricky business in a closeup. The most famous example of looping was Hugh Hudson's excellent film, *Greystoke: The Legend of Tarzan, Lord of the Apes*. Andie MacDowell, playing Jane, had a heavy southern accent that could not be entirely disguised, so Glenn Close was hired to re-voice the entire role. I have seen this film three times and never suspected a thing.

TODD-AO
GLEN GLENN
s t u d i o s
"*Miss Evers Boys*"   HBO-NY
AUTOMATED DIALOGUE REPLACEMENT CUE SHEET

R- 2

1/3/97   Page:_**5**_ of _**27**_

	CHARACTER	START/ STOP	NOTES	CHANNELS 9 10 11 12 13 14 15 16	DIALOGUE
2001.	Douglas	02:00:14:25 02:00:16:20			We'll have to test them first of course......
2002.	Douglas	02:00:16:20 02:00:18:27			Give them wassermans to make sure. I'll take that.
2003.	Brodus	02:00:18:22 02:00:21:10			Doctor, that in itself would be a huge undertaking.
2004.	Douglas	02:00:21:29 02:00:23:26			Great pains for great rewards. Right?
2005.	Brodus	02:00:23:29 02:00:27:20			You don't intend on them they have syphilis do you?
2006.	Douglas	02:00:28:10 02:00:31:04			Well if they have it we'll have to tell them something won't we?
2007.	Miss Evers	02:00:31:23 02:00:35:02			Well, *maybe we better not use a name they never heard before..........*
2008.	Miss Evers	02:00:35:02 02:00:37:01			That'll just scare them off doctor.
2009.	GROUP	02:00:37:28 02:01:04:20			(HOSPITAL CORRIDOR WALLA)
2010.	GROUP	02:01:04:20 02:02:06:06			(HOSPITAL WARD WALLA)
2011.	Miss Evers	02:01:33:08 02:01:38:07			And that new man that's come in, you check him for a fever every two hours and make sure he don't go spiking on you.
2012.	GROUP	02:02:06:06 02:02:16:14			(COURTROOM WALLA)
2013.	Miss Evers	02:02:17:03 02:02:20:27			I've been sent here by... I've been sent here by the.....
2014.	GROUP MAN	02:03:09:15 02:03:34:10			(SIGHS & GRUNTS)

FIGURE 11.1   An ADR list. This and Figure 11.2, are from *Miss Evers' Boys* and were prepared by supervising sound editor Richard Taylor of Todd-A-O.

If the production dialogue track has problems that cannot be fixed by looping, it may be efficient to do a **dialogue pre-dub** to produce a clean dialogue track (**dub** is short for "doubling" and originally referred only to the final mix, although now it refers generically to almost any kind of re-recording).

Prelays

A number of sound sources are developed before the final mix that provide sound materials of various kinds: these are called the **prelays**. One comes from the **Foley** artists (named after the person who developed the technique), who produce footsteps, glass clinks, door sounds, and other specific sounds that must be synchronized to the picture. Another comes from the unseen, unsung sound editors who prepare general sound effects such as rain, thunder, and animal and traffic noises. Yet another prelay comes from groups of actors who are brought in to provide the **walla** of background conversations, telephone voices, and other vocal embellishments. Such specialists are called "looping groups."

Special attention is paid to any music in the show that is not part of the composed score. This is called **source music**, such as radios or juke boxes playing in the background, and any songs sung by the actors; rights must be procured for all such music. There are two types of music rights, both of which must be purchased: the *master rights* cover a specific version of a song by a specific artist on a specific record, and the *publishing rights*, which are for the original music and lyrics regardless of who performs it. These rights can be quite costly, from $10,000 for a song used under a scene to $30,000 for one featured as part of the titles. Like older books and plays, older music, such as traditional gospel songs, may be in the public domain and do not require the purchase of rights. For independent films, some music may be made available with a nonprofit release that permits showings at festivals and for other nonprofit purposes.

To help avoid the cost of rights for source music, composers will sometimes be asked to write **"sounds like"** music. A good composer can mimic any kind of music using melodies of his or her own invention, thus requiring no rights. This music is recorded along with the rest of the score and used with filtration to substitute for radio or phonograph music.

Depending on the scope of the show's needs, sound is a significant portion of the post-production budget. Sometimes, sound will be contracted as a package, meaning that the sound facility agrees to supply everything needed (except the score) for a flat fee. A 1-hour episodic television show might cost $25,000 to $40,000; a television movie from $60,000 to $150,000; a feature film $400,000 or more.

Music

A composer may have been hired during an earlier stage of Post and has perhaps already seen the director's cut and the evolving versions of the edited picture, although often the composer will join the team only after the cut is locked. The director, the producer, and the creative executive will have discussed the music (also called the **underscore**) in general terms, and the

Production: <u>MISS EVERS' BOYS</u>
MUSIC SPOTTING NOTES
Thursday, January 2, 1997

REEL 1   (3 Starts)
1m1   2:20.94
   c1:00:33:26
   c1:02:54:20
Main Title

"MAIN TITLE (VOCAL)"
MUSIC IN on CENTER DISS to group in cotton field
MUSIC tails under Evers VO

1m2   9.18
   c1:06:56:09
   c1:07:05:14
Background Instrumental

"Hallelujah"
MUSIC IN as Ms Evers lifts head to look at Doctor Brodus (after taking
fluid from young boys chest)//CUT to EXT DAY road thru town//Ms
Evers VO, "This morning when the reverend was talking about
miracles..."//CUT car driving by//MUSIC TAILS on CUT to 2 shot of
Ms Evers & her father walking toward us

1m3s   1:29.16
   c1:08:34:14
   c1:10:03:16
Composer Source

"Blues Town"
MUSIC IN on CUT to Dr. Douglas
MUSIC OUT on CUT to INT Car

(Period Blues Source)

REEL 2   (3 Starts)
2m1   1:48.91
   c2:02:16:14
   c2:04:05:08
Background Instrumental

"Ms Evers' Mission"
MUSIC IN on CUT to Ms Evers driving down road//CUT Evers in
car//CUT Evers talking to group about getting medicine//CUT Evers
talking to cotton grower//CUT Evers talking to group in cotton
field//MUSIC OUT under production harmonica

(G.P.s on & around Evers as she speaks to different groups - Maybe an
a capella piece)

2m2s   53.32
   c2:04:05:08
   c2:04:58:16
Production Source

"Production Harmonica"
MUSIC IN over group in cotton field
MUSIC OUT on foot stomp in school house

(Production Source pre-recorded - MUSIC needs some editing)

2m3   49.28
   c2:08:27:21
   c2:09:16:28
Background Instrumental

"Caleb's Theme"
MUSIC IN as Evers raises her head in realization//She stands and looks
at desk behind her//She talks with other men//CUT to Evers
walking//CUT to Caleb working on truck engine//MUSIC OUT as Evers
slaps Caleb

FIGURE 11.2   A music spotting list.

composer will have already submitted sample thematic material recorded on a synthesizer, so that a general approach has been agreed upon. At the music spotting session, the director will identify the location and duration of the specific cues (see Fig. 11.2). Director Sydney Pollack describes spotting with the composer:

> We watch the movie, discussing in great detail the texture of the music and where it should be placed. . . . It gets very specific. We might decide, "Start the music when she turns her head there and continue to the point where he walks out the door." That calls for a music cue that is exactly 130 feet 6 frames in length. The **music editor** creates a master log of all these choices and times. Then the composer goes off to write the score.[2]

Although experienced film composers work amazingly fast, even they are usually rushed to finish before (sometimes just days before) the final mix. Television scores are often written in just 3 or 4 weeks, and feature films may take twice as long. Composers often write on a synthesizer keyboard while watching a videotape of the show; this special tape has been prepared by the music editor (composers and music editors are usually a team). It displays the "in" and "out" of every cue as established at the spotting session.

Film composers are often contracted to supply an entire **music package**, meaning that for one set price they pay studio rentals, musician salaries, and all other costs necessary to deliver finished tapes for the final mix; such packages can range from as little as $30,000 to hundreds of thousands, with $60,000 being an average for television movies.

The composer may do the orchestrations or may utilize the services of a separate orchestrator. The orchestral scores are prepared by a manuscripter (there are computer programs to assist in this). The necessary musicians are hired by the **orchestra contractor**. A recording stage with equipment and services of a recording engineer is rented. All is now ready for the **scoring session**.

The musicians arrive and find the microphones already placed by the engineer. The sections of the orchestra are on separate microphones, sometimes with barriers between them to provide isolation; solo instruments are often placed in an adjoining booth and separated completely from the rest of the orchestra. This gives the mixer the ability to establish a properly balanced sound. Because these tracks are kept separate, they may be manipulated later to alter the content of a cue.

The session is usually conducted by the composer as he or she watches the music editor's tape on a monitor. The live orchestra is augmented by a pre-recorded electronic source that is created on a synthesizer and controlled by the music editor. Most film scores are a mixture of both acoustic and electronic sources, although there are some instruments that the computer does not mimic well, such as woodwinds. However, the computer is getting better and better at mimicking live players, and cost can be reduced by using more "machine" and fewer live musicians.

The tapes from the scoring session are carefully prepared (sometimes overnight) by the music editor, who synchronizes them to the picture on a time-coded master tape. They are now ready to take their place in the final mix.

The Final Mix

With all the sound elements now in hand, the director, the producer, the editor, the composer, the music editor, and the supervising sound editor gather on a **dubbing stage**. Here they work with two or three mixers to blend dialogue, effects, and music to produce the final mix of the show. The mixers sit at a large mixing board, with the lead mixer (who handles the dialogue) in the center, the effects mixer on his or her right, and the music mixer (if any) on the left. The efficiency of digital sound control has reduced the need for three mixers, so almost all mixes are now done by two persons, with one handling both music and effects. On the dubbing stage, the locked cut is projected on a large screen with the frame numbers displayed below it; the movie is broken into reels, each of which holds approximately 11 minutes worth of film and the mix proceeds reel-by-reel.

The prelays form a foundation for the mix. Every moment of the film is repeated over and over, and the elements are adjusted in relation to one another. The dialogue must be easily understandable against the effects and music. The effects are manipulated and placed to achieve not only realism but also dramatic emphasis (the famous taxicab scene in Elia Kazan's *On the Waterfront*, for example, is beautifully punctuated by horn honks and other environmental sound effects). The music cues, now that they can be heard in the flow of the picture and in relation to all the other elements, may, if necessary, be manipulated to change their quality, lengthen or, shorten them, or reshape them, or even to place them differently within the show. The music editor can accomplish such adjustments fairly quickly using sophisticated computer programs. Music cues can also be altered by utilizing the isolation of the various musical elements on separate tracks; for instance, the violins might be softened, or one of the other instruments might be featured. Although they are mixed to achieve a single overall effect, the three elements (dialogue, music, and effects) are actually recorded separately, because they must be separated later. The final mix lasts anywhere from 3 days for a simple television movie to many weeks for a complicated feature. Features are mixed in theater-size dubbing stages and sometimes an audience will be brought in so that the mix can be heard under actual theater conditions.

Although the director has the final say during the mix, the completed mix is always reviewed by the executives of the network or studio. They often give notes, and they have the right to change the mix if they wish. Once the mix is approved, the entire show is **laid back** by the sound mixer and editor to marry the three elements and to double-check the synchronization.

At the same time, a version of the mix is prepared that has only the music and effects and no dialogue; this is called the **M & E** and is used by foreign distributors to insert foreign language translations of the dialogue. Another version may be prepared with only dialogue and effects and no music (**D & E**); this is used to create trailers and other promotional materials that, after editing, may be given their own music.

As film recording and theater sound systems have been enhanced by new technology, the mix has become a more and more important aspect of many films. Even television movies, condemned to be heard over the woefully inadequate speakers in most television sets, now often get complex mixes because of the possibility of foreign theatrical release, Surround-Sound broadcasting, and DVD or home video. One of the most popular mixing formats today is called *5.1*. It involves three front channels (left, center, right) and two rear "surround" channels. The ".1" stands for the subwoofer, a huge speaker that can literally shake the theater. Although the cost of mixing has increased as mixes have become more complex, the money spent here is handsomely repaid in the enhanced effectiveness of the final product.

Summary

Only when the cut is locked can work begin on sound because all music, effects, and dialogue are synchronized to picture; the supervising sound editor assumes leadership of some aspects of the project. The first step is the spotting session when the director "spots" the effects. Unusable dialogue is replaced by looping (ADR). Various prelays are prepared: one is the Foley, in which specific sounds are synchronized to picture; another provides general sound effects; yet another comes from the "loop group" that is brought in to provide the "walla." At the music spotting session, the director and the composer discuss the nature and placement of the music. Shortly before the final mix, the scoring session is held, conducted by the composer.

With all sound elements now in hand, the production team gathers on a dubbing stage where two or three mixers blend dialogue, effects, and music to produce the final mix of the show. When approved by the network or studio, the entire show is laid back, and a version is prepared for foreign use with only the music and effects (M & E).

NOTES

1. Sydney Pollack, in *The Movie Business Book*, ed. Jason E. Squire, Fireside (New York, 1992), p. 50.
2. Ibid.

12 Post III

Printing, Delivery, and Distribution

After the final mix, a number of technical steps remain to complete the film-making process, after which the film is ready for delivery and distribution. The first of these steps is to prepare the negative for printing, and, as we noted in the previous chapter, this process actually started when the cut was locked, well before the final mix.

Negative Cutting and Timing

As soon as the cut is locked, the **negative cutter** begins work. The assistant editor prints out a *negative cut list* from the editing system computer; this list provides the frame numbers printed on the film itself for every cut. Guided by these numbers, the negative cutter takes the original negatives, untouched since the dailies were made, and splices them onto two reels, the **A and B rolls**. Needless to say, a mistake in cutting that injures the original negative is a disaster of major proportions and negative cutters work with great care in a dust-free environment. Additional negatives prepared by the **optical house** for titles, dissolves, and other optical effects are inserted in the appropriate places on the A and B rolls. When the #2 rolls are run simultaneously through a printing machine, the alternating shots on the A and B rolls combine to produce the seamless flow of the **composite print**.

The printing machine is controlled by a computer and can adjust the source light, shot by shot, to create different exposures and color balance. As we have said, this process is called timing. The timing process has two aims: to fulfill the look of the film as intended by the DP and director and to produce the right visual flow from cut to cut and scene to scene. Most good DPs insist (and have it in their contracts) that they must supervise the timing process, because subtle adjustments can radically alter the look of the film. Left to their own devices, many studios and networks want a "safe" result and tend to produce prints and video transfers that are too light and lacking in character.

The timing process begins with the striking of an initial print called a *first trial*. This print is *mute*, as are all those used for timing; sound will be rejoined to picture only at the end of the timing process. The first trial is viewed by the DP and sometimes also by the director, the editor, the producer, and the post-production supervisor. As careful as the DP may have been in setting exposures during the Shoot, because the various scenes were shot at different times under different light conditions, there may be variations in color, brightness, and density from shot to shot. The DP works closely with the **timer** to adjust each shot, making it either lighter ("printed up") or darker ("printed down") or to intensify or diminish specific colors ("warming" or "cooling" the shot). The aim is not only to make the visual flow smooth, but also to enhance the mood of each scene.

Based on the notes given on the first trial, another print is made. Several trial prints may be needed, and each costs thousands of dollars. (There is a cheaper alternative to trial printing in which representative frames from each scene are printed individually; these *key frames* are viewed in succession like a slide show. Although this is a less effective method of timing, it can suffice for a low-budget film.) After one or more trials, a final version is printed for approval by the DP, the director, the producer, and the studio or network; this is called the **answer print**.

The original negative is now used to print an interpositive (**IP**) from which an internegative (**IN**) is made. The internegative will be used for all future printing, and the precious original cut negative is retired to storage where it remains safe from the rigors of the printing process.

Finally, for theatrical film, the results of the final sound mix is transferred to an **optical soundtrack** that is printed on the internegative in a strip alongside the picture. All is now ready for the striking of **release prints**.

For television broadcast, either the IP, the IN, or (rarely) the original negative is used to do a *video transfer*. Again, the DP works closely with a *video timer*, and the timing process happens all over again. In fact, today's highly sophisticated video transfer systems permit an even more subtle and complex set of adjustments than does film timing, including the timing of separate zones within the frame. For example, I recently produced a movie in which we had to reshoot an outdoor scene. The original scene had been shot on a sunny day with a clear blue sky, but on the day of the reshoot the sky was gray and overcast. We had to go ahead, but were worried about the match between the reshot scene and the scenes that preceded and followed it. As usual, the decision was to "fix it in Post." In the film timing, the DP was able to "warm up" the reshot scene enough to make it almost match the adjoining sunny scenes, but because the entire frame was made warmer, the sky ended up looking very gray. When the video transfer was made, however, the sky could be separately timed and came out a wonderful blue.

If and when film is replaced by digital sources, this kind of freedom to manipulate the image will create infinite possibilities. (More on this in the next chapter.)

Final Delivery

The completed film must now be accepted by the network or studio for **delivery**. The producer has been given a long list of *delivery requirements* that specifies the form in which the film must be delivered for release or broadcast. The main delivery elements, of course, are the negative, the IN, the videotape master, and the M&E audio tracks for foreign use. Also required are a large number of supporting documents. These usually include:

- The chain of title proving ownership of any underlying sources, script, and the film itself;
- A spotted dialogue list or continuity script; these must be "as broadcast" because they will be used with the M&E tracks to translate and dub foreign versions;
- Copies of the research report and all clearances and releases. These will be essential for E&O insurance.
- The music scores and cue sheets;
- Biographies of key personnel for publicity use;
- Complete cast and crew credits, deal memos, and contracts.

The mountain of production paperwork and accounting information, as well as the dailies and outtakes, are boxed and sent to storage. Only when the delivery is complete in every detail will the producer receive his or her final payment.

After delivery, the stars, director, and producers will sometimes participate in the marketing and distribution campaign conducted by the studio or network. They attend press presentations and premieres. The producers make submissions for festivals and awards such as the Emmy or Oscars. If fortunate enough to be nominated, he or she may have to attend award ceremonies, since awards are usually given to individuals rather than to networks or studios.

Independent Marketing and Distribution

For independent filmmakers, the end of the production process is the beginning of a whole new phase of work. Unless they have arranged a distribution deal as part of their financing, they must now sell their film to a distributor. This process begins with a publicity campaign aimed at creating a "buzz" for the film. An attractive press kit with photos, a synopsis, and bios is a starting point; it can be used to generate articles in the press and in magazines aimed at the indie film market (such as *Filmmaker* and *The Independent Film and Video Monthly*). A well-organized premiere can attract celebrities and press. A website can be set up; a trailer can be cut and offered on the Internet.

Entry into the Independent Feature Film Market (IFFM) held annually in New York is a must, as is entry in various festivals such as Sundance, Berlin, Cannes, and Venice, as well as Toronto and New York; there are dozens of others, all of which can help bring attention to an indie and provide it with prestigious credits and reviews.

It was once nearly impossible to find wide distribution for independent features, and they were condemned to the limited revenue of "art theaters." Now, however, there are savvy distributors who have realized that properly marketed indies can make substantial profits. There are currently six main indie distributors, listed here with a few of their films: Miramax (*Sling Blade, Pulp Fiction, The Crying Game*), Fine Line (*Shine, Hoop Dreams, The Player*), Fox Searchlight (*The Brothers McMullen, The Full Monty, Star Maps*), October Films (*Secrets & Lies, Breaking the Waves*), Sony Picture Classics (*Lone Star, Mi Vida Loca, Welcome to the Dollhouse*), and Gramercy (*The Usual Suspects, Dead Man Walking, Fargo*). In addition, there are more than a dozen smaller companies that also handle indies.

Perhaps one of the most important factors in an indie distribution deal is how much money the company is willing to commit to the upfront costs for distribution prints and advertising, called simply **P & A**. A $250,000 commitment from a small distributor or $500,000 from one of the "major indies" is a good figure for an initial release. If the picture is well received in this first limited release, most companies will begin to expand their P&A expenditures, putting the movie into wider and wider release. This gradual expansion of distribution as the film's momentum grows was the strategy that broke open the indie market for early hits such as *Fried Green Tomatoes*.

Although the major studios occasionally try to make and market low-budget films, their huge marketing departments are geared to promoting blockbusters, which often cost as much to sell and distribute as they do to make; as a result, when a major studio tries to sell a low budget film, it is like trying to drive a thumbtack with a sledgehammer. There have been a few notable exceptions: Warner Brothers, for example, was successful in marketing *Roger & Me* (which they bought for $3 million) and *Stand and Deliver* (which cost them $5 million).

If an indie filmmaker has not pre-sold domestic video or key foreign markets as part of his or her financing, these may now be sold, although only films that have had some form of domestic theatrical release will fetch good prices. Some premium cable outlets such as *Cinemax* show indies, and pay fairly well, although their deals are predicated on the film's theatrical success and the presence of name actors. The three independent film cable networks, *Bravo*, *The Independent Film Channel* (IFC), and *The Sundance Film Channel*, are the most open to indies, even those that have never been released theatrically; exposure and license fees on these outlets for unreleased films, however, are minuscule: $10,000 to $40,000 for a 2- or 3-year exclusive term.

The Internet will surely have a massive effect on the indie market, not to mention the entertainment industry as a whole. As author Gregg Merritt says,

> The onslaught of the information highway will be changing all the rules for video and television, and for theatrical distribution as well. With the click of a keystroke, consumers around the world will be able to activate state-of-the-art high-definition screens with digital sound, showing them any movie they wish to see . . . When this day arrives, video stores will be on their way out . . . television scheduling will be altered—or become obsolete; even theaters will be rocked to their foundations. How royalties will be paid when someone downloads your movie in Chicago or Bombay is a question yet to be answered. But one thing is for sure: independent film distribution will never be the same.[1]

The fight over royalties has already begun. The WGA and SAG are fighting the studios and networks over cable residuals, and the recording industry is trying to stop the free distribution of music over the Internet. Broad band transmission will no doubt someday make home distribution of films common, although I doubt if we will stop seeing films in theaters anymore than we did after the advent of television. In any case, if the questions of copyright and royalty payments from these new forms of distribution can be resolved, they will bode well for independent filmmakers. (The impact of digital filmmaking will be discussed in the next chapter.)

In the face of these new possibilities, we end this chapter with advice from Henry Jaglom, an independent writer-director whose films include *Tracks*, *Can She Bake a Cherry Pie?*, *Eating*, and *Venice/Venice*. Over the years, he has developed a loyal audience that represents 10% to 15% of the American movie-going public. He set up his own distribution company and now finances and successfully distributes his own films both domestically and in foreign markets. His method is simple: He keeps his budgets below $1 million but attracts big name actors such as Jack Nicholson, Dennis Hopper, and Karen Black by giving them meaningful profit participation. He raises nearly all of a film's budget by pre-selling key European markets; then, owning the negative, he distributes his film through his own releasing company to art theaters in various cities, to a home video distributor, and in the remaining overseas markets. He even publishes book versions of his movies and sells T-shirts in the theaters. He makes an excellent profit, as much as $3.5 million on a $1 million film, and is now able to keep complete control over his pictures.

My advice to new filmmakers is quite simple: *Do not accept anyone's word that something is impossible* . . . To make a movie, you need as much money as you've got, not a penny more. If it's just $20,000 you can raise, take a video camera and go make a movie.[2]

Summary

As soon as the cut is locked, the negative cutter begins work. Guided by the cut list that was produced by the editing system, he or she splices the negatives onto two reels, the A and B rolls. Negatives prepared by the optical house for titles, dissolves, and other optical effects are inserted as needed. A first trial print is struck, and the DP works closely with the film timer to adjust each shot to make the visual flow smooth and to enhance the mood of each scene. Finally, an answer print is produced. The original negative is now used to print an interpositive (IP) from which an internegative (IN) is made and used for all future printing. The optical soundtrack is added for theater use, and the DP works closely with the video timer to transfer the show for video broadcast.

After meeting the requirements for final delivery, the stars, director, and producer may be called on to participate in the picture's exploitation. An independent filmmaker, however, must now sell his or her film into distribution. This requires developing interest in the film through the press, screenings, and festivals, until a distribution deal can be made. There are several companies that specialize in picking up indie films and know how to give them effective marketing and distribution, beginning with a substantial commitment to prints and advertising (P & A). Home video, foreign distribution, and cable TV are other potential markets.

The whole arena of home distribution through the Internet will open new horizons for the indie filmmaker if the questions of copyright and royalty payments can be resolved.

NOTES

1. Greg Merritt, *Film Production: The Complete Uncensored Guide to Independent Filmmaking*, Lone Eagle Publishing, Los Angeles, 1988, p. 221.
2. Henry Jaglom, in *The Movie Business Book*, ed. Jason E. Squire, Fireside (New York, 1992), p. 81.

CHAPTER

13 High Definition Video

Toward Filmless Filmmaking

Recent technological advances in high-definition digital video (**HD**) have made filmless filmmaking a reality. Several feature films have been shot in HD (most notably George Lucas' *Star Wars: Episode II*) as well as several television series (such as *Diagnosis Murder*). Major companies such as Sony and Panavision are investing large sums in its development, and several networks are now requiring that MOWs be delivered in HD rather than film.

There were some esthetic objections to HD when it was first introduced. Earlier forms of HD looked too "hard" or "cold" to many filmmakers. Even some HD proponents wondered if the extreme sharpness of the HD picture might not be distracting; one asked, "does enjoying the story require being able to read the labels on the cans in the background?" Some die-hards even missed filmic qualities that might be considered defects: "motion blur" caused by fast-moving objects, "graininess" in low-light situations, and "jitter" caused by the movement of the film through the gate. However, the newest generations of HD have answered these complaints. The HD image can now be rendered virtually indistinguishable from film.

Whether HD fulfills its promise and becomes the main way that theatrical films are made and displayed, and the dominant format for broadcast television, will depend on whether several technological and political issues can be resolved. To understand the advantages and disadvantages of HD compared to film and standard television, you must understand the fundamental differences between them: first, how each captures the image itself; second, how each achieves the appearance of motion; and third, their technical differences of format and process.

Capturing the Image

Film stock captures an image by a *chemical* process. Light passing through the camera lens falls on the film and activates tiny grains of chemicals contained in the film emulsion. In color film, these grains are laid in layers, each layer reacting to one of the three primary colors (in film processing the actual colors used are cyan, magenta, and yellow). Very fine-grain films produce extremely sharp images (i.e., they produce a higher level of **resolution**) but they require more light, therefore fine-grain films are said to be "slower." Film stock is constantly being improved to provide high resolution at faster speeds, but when the amount of light is inadequate the picture becomes "grainy."

Video, however, records an image by an *electrical* process. A sensor scans the image coming through the lens and converts it to an electrical signal. In standard analog television, this signal is transmitted via waves of varying size and shape. In *digital* television, it is converted (digitized) into a series of individual on/off commands called a *bitstream*. In the projector or TV set, these commands are translated into dots of light called **pixels**. These pixels are laid down along fine lines by a scanning electron beam. The recreated image can then be projected directly onto a theater screen, onto a television screen, or onto film stock. When a video is shot in inadequate light, or is enlarged too much, instead of becoming "grainy" as does film, it "pixelates" into little blocks of color.

Increasing the number of pixels within the video frame increases the level of resolution and produces the high-definition video picture. Ordinary broadcast television has a definition of 720 × 480, meaning that there are 720 pixels on 480 lines. The best HD in common use, by comparison, has a definition of 1920 × 1035. Simple multiplication tells you that the standard television frame has about 350,000 pixels, and HD has almost 2 million, six times as many. (You can easily see the difference in these levels of resolution by changing the display properties on a computer.)

How high is the definition of high-definition video compared to film? It is hard to quantify the difference. The grains of chemicals suspended in film emulsion are distributed randomly, whereas the pixels in a video frame are distributed evenly on a grid of horizontal and vertical lines. This makes a fundamental visual difference between them, and a direct comparison is a bit misleading. However, engineers tell me that to create a digital image that is as sharp as the sharpest film, you would need about 12 million pixels per frame (roughly 4000 × 3000). It is, in fact, possible to produce a video image that is even sharper than the sharpest film, but this technology, used in spy satellites and scientific research, requires the storage of huge quantities of data and is impractical for most ordinary purposes. The best digital photographic cameras now on sale operate at about 3 million pixels, and the best digital movie cameras currently in use operate at about 2 million pixels per frame.

Although this would seem to mean that a 2 million-pixel digital video movie frame is only one sixth as sharp as its 12 million-pixel film counterpart, this is not the case in practice. A digital image can be reproduced infinitely without any change, but a film image degrades (loses resolution) every time it is reproduced. The film distribution process, moreover, requires making copies of copies, each of these being one more "generation" removed from the original negative. The film image you see in your local theater is at least four generations away from the negative: The original negative is used to make an answer print, from which an interpositive (IP) is made to produce an internegative (IN), and this is used to strike the release prints you see. By the time it reaches you, the film image has degraded to a resolution equivalent to a video image of about—you guessed it—2 million pixels. I have watched film and HD side by side, and I cannot tell the difference on the basis of resolution; if anything, the HD image seems sharper.

The Illusion of Motion

Besides the different ways that film and video record the image, there are some differences in the way they achieve the illusion of motion. As most people know, the illusion of motion in both film and video is created from a sequence of still pictures (**frames**). When the sequence of frames runs fast enough, our brain sees it as flowing motion because of a phenomenon called "the persistence of vision." As the number of frames per second (called the **frame rate**) is increased, the illusion of motion is enhanced.

When Thomas Edison first constructed his motion picture camera using film invented by George Eastman, it ran at 48 frames per second. This produced a very smooth moving image, but it consumed too much film. To solve this problem, one of Edison's assistants developed a camera shutter with three blades, so that the frame rate dropped to one third of 48, or 16 frames per second. This was the slowest frame rate that maintained an acceptable illusion of motion, although it was this slower frame rate that gave the early silent films their "flicker" (which is why movies are still called "flicks"). When "talkies" were developed, it was found that the sound track could not be properly synchronized at this low frame rate, therefore a two-bladed shutter was adopted, resulting in today's frame rate of one half of 48, or 24 frames per second. A few high-speed film formats have been developed, such as the 60-frame-per-second Showscan, but because of the large amounts of film required these have proven impractical.

Video also has a frame rate, which is the number of times per second that the image is scanned. When video was developed, the movie frame rate of 24 frames per second was found to produce a jerky video picture, especially for fast motion as in sporting events. The video frame rate was therefore increased to 30 frames per second, at which point the motion was sufficiently smooth. In standard video, motion is made even smoother by scanning each frame twice, once to capture the even-numbered lines, and again to fill in the odd-numbered lines. This **interlaced video** is still the common broadcast standard.

The differential between 30-frame video and 24-frame film requires that when transferring from film to video, six frames must be added to each second of film. This is accomplished by duplicating some frames through a process called a "3:2 pulldown." Recently, however, 24-frame video has been developed which produces smooth motion. It scans each frame only once, each line in sequence, and is called *24-frame progressive video*, or simply **24p**. 24p HD produces a picture that rivals film in appearance, and can be transferred to film without altering the frame rate. Editing and other aspects of post-production are greatly simplified by the advent of 24p, and its proponents say that once you have a 24p master, you can fairly easily generate any other format imaginable.

Aspect Ratios

Another important difference between film and HD is the shape of the frame itself. When Thomas Edison developed his camera, he chose a frame that was three units high by four units wide ("3 by 4"). This proportion of frame height to width is called the **aspect ratio** and is usually expressed as a number, which in this case is 1.33:1 (one-third wider than high). Edison's aspect ratio became the standard for all films until 1953, when 20th Century Fox brought out the biblical epic *The Robe* in CinemaScope. Other "wide-screen" formats soon followed, and the use of stereophonic sound also became widespread. CinemaScope remains the widest aspect ratio in use at 2.35:1 (two and one-third times wider than high). Wide formats require a special type of lens on both cameras and projectors that permit the wide image to be compressed onto a normal film frame then uncompressed when projected. For this reason, these formats are called **anamorphic**. Edison's old ratio of 1.33:1, however, remains the standard for ordinary broadcast television (Figure 13.1). Although CinemaScope itself is rarely used nowadays because it requires a special screen, and because it is difficult to compose shots in such an extremely wide format, most feature films are shot in more moderately wide-screen format, either the "Standard Academy" ratio of 1.85:1, or the "Foreign Theatrical" standard of 1.66:1.

HD systems are also wide-screen, but use an altogether different aspect ratio of 1.78:1 (three-fourths wider than it is high), which is also called "16 by 9." This is midway between Standard Academy and Foreign Theatrical, and is considerably wider than standard TV. Television shows being shot in HD (e.g., the CBS program *CSI: Crime Scene Investigation*) may be broadcast in both 1.78:1 and 1.33:1. The problem for the DP and director is to block and

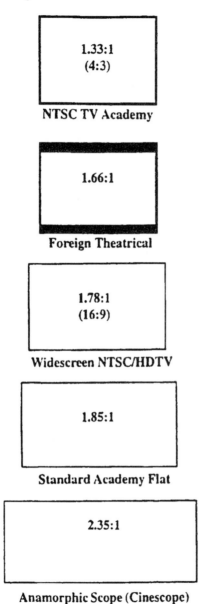

FIGURE 13.1   Aspect ratios. The second screen is "letter boxed" in the way many feature films are broadcast on standard television to avoid "panning" and "scanning" within the frame.

compose shots that work in both the wide and the narrowest aspect ratios simultaneously, a difficult task. (When a 16 × 9 picture is viewed on an ordinary 3 × 4 television set, it is sometimes "letterboxed.")

Shooting in HD

The development of 24p HD has greatly encouraged HD production. At first there were only a few prototypical cameras with a limited complement of lenses in existence, and filmmakers had to borrow them from manufacturers. At this writing, there are still only about 30 24p HD cameras available for rent in Los Angeles, but Panavision has ordered 100 more that they will outfit with a full range of lenses for rental purposes in 2001.

The first thing you notice on an HD shoot is the somewhat smaller camera. Whereas early HD cameras (like ordinary broadcast television cameras) had to be connected to their recorder by an "umbilical cord," the current HD camera is self-contained. It is loaded with a book-size cartridge capable of storing about 40 minutes of digital material (considerably more than the largest film load). This means that shooting is interrupted less to reload the camera.

It also means that there is no film stock to buy, no waste of unused "short ends" on the film rolls, and no handling and shipping of bulky film containers. Because the digital camera has no moving parts, many of the mechanical problems of film cameras are eliminated. There is also no need to develop film overnight, or telecine to video in order to create dailies. HD dailies are instantaneous and a well-calibrated monitor can show the filmmakers exactly what they've shot on the spot, virtually eliminating the need for re-shoots. While shooting, the HD camera can be kept running more freely than in film because costly film stock is not being consumed; mistakes can simply be erased. The time HD saves on the set can afford the luxury of more takes.

HD can save time in other ways as well. Though lighting must be done with the same care as in film, it can be done using less wattage because the video camera is far more sensitive to light than even the fastest film stock. This means that less lighting equipment needs to be rented, transported, and adjusted. In all, there are many advantages to shooting in HD, but certain special precautions must be taken. Crews familiar with HD are scarce, and an engineer must usually be added to the crew to handle the programming of the camera and the calibration of the monitor. Because the monitor has usually only a 14-inch screen, it is possible for a shot that is slightly out of focus to slip by if the replays are not scrutinized carefully. Also, the DP must be familiar with the fundamental differences between lighting for film and for HD. Film can lose detail in dark areas, but HD loses detail in bright areas.

Although shadows in film can sometimes be lightened to retrieve the information in them, overly bright areas in HD simply contain no information and cannot be adjusted in Post. For this reason, shooting in bright sunlight is the most demanding situation for the HD DP.

In practice, HD requires that dailies must still be made; these contain only the **circled takes** (those chosen to be printed by the director) and have time code added (a flex file) for editing purposes. These HD dailies, however, are considerably cheaper than film dailies to produce because they involve no film processing.

HD in Post

There are potential time and cost savings associated with HD in Post and distribution. First, the material from the set can be put directly into the editing system without first being digitized. Editing systems have been developed that work directly with HD material, and it is also possible to temporarily compress the HD material to a lower level of resolution and use it in standard non-linear editing systems.

If the final product is delivered in video, there are further savings from the elimination of film negative cutting, the creation of opticals for fades, titles, and film printing costs. These factors by themselves may save over $175,000 on a 90-minute feature film. However, if the final product must be transferred from video to film for distribution purposes, some of these savings will be lost, since video-to-film transfer is presently a fairly expensive process. A high quality scan takes about 6 seconds per frame, and the cost totals about $60,000 or more for an average full-length film.

Editing in HD gives a truer reading of what the final product will look like; when editing with standard video, it is easy to miss details, such as slightly soft focus or distracting background elements, and these can loom very large when the film is finally projected (there is a shot of a period street in *Miss Evers' Boys* that has modern streetlights in the far background; these were never noticed until the film was completed and projected). The recent Coen Brothers' film, *O Brother Where Art Thou*, was shot in film, transferred to a digital intermediate for editing, then transferred back to film (a process that avoided the costs of cutting the film negative).

Color timing is much more flexible in HD than in film, and it is possible to make extraordinary adjustments that would not be possible in film. For example, in one recent HD film the color of a character's sweater was changed in several scenes. If necessary, even more radical changes are possible; in the recent HBO film *For Love or Country*, a shot was digitized to remove an entire bus from the background. And the "dirt" that plagues film processing (scratches, blotches, dust, and hair) is nonexistent in HD.

Although HD is used for restoring and archiving films in long-term storage, it is a myth that HD "lasts forever." Even the best digital storage techniques will last only a decade or so, and digital archives must be renewed by making a fresh copy at least that often. The refreshed copy, of course, is indistinguishable from the original, so in this sense HD can last forever. Color film stock, on the other hand, inevitably yellows and loses quality with age. (The very best long-term storage of color film is achieved by separating the three primary colors through the use of filters, which reduces each to a series of black-and-white images. These are then recorded on alternating frames of a single strip of black-and-white film. When printed, the process is reversed to restore the color.)

HD Distribution

The distribution of theatrical films in HD is still years away, but would be a tremendous economic advantage. The major studios currently spend about $2 billion a year making prints and shipping them, and prints wear out fairly quickly. In a digital world, movies would be transmitted directly to theaters. (The Fox studio recently experimented with sending the film *Titan AE* to a theater in Georgia over the Internet, but the quality of the transmission was poor; eventually it is more likely that HD distribution will be achieved by satellite rather than by land lines.) HD distribution would also reduce the most common form of piracy, which occurs when film prints are "lent" for "midnight telecine" (a projectionist was recently arrested for receiving $10,000 to loan a print of *Star Wars* for a few hours to an outfit that had a crude telecine unit mounted in a van).

HD projection systems capable of filling the largest theater screens have recently been developed, though they are costly; the smaller screens in most multiplex theaters are already within range of relatively inexpensive digital projectors. At this writing, there are 31 digital theaters in regular operation in the United States and several private screening theaters. The biggest obstacle to the general adoption of digital projection is the high cost of converting theaters from film to video projection systems (as much as $150,000 per screen). The distributors expect the theater owners (exhibitors) to bear the cost of the conversion, but the exhibitors argue that since HD saves the distributors so much money, they should bear the cost. The argument rages on, but I have heard predictions that by 2010, half the movies shown in American theaters will be projected in HD.

While the problems of projecting HD in theaters are being resolved, more and more movies are being shot in HD and transferred to film for distribution. Recent films such as *Timecode, The Celebration, The Buena Vista Social Club,* and *The Blair Witch Project* have been shot in this way, and **digital-to-film** is becoming a popular production format. Sony has the leading technology for the transfer of digital-to-film in its Electron Beam Recorder (originally developed for restoration and archival purposes) though there are other, less expensive systems that produce excellent results, such as that developed by Laser Pacific, the inventors of the 24p camera.

HD at Home

One obstacle to the adoption of HD as a television broadcast standard is that several different HD formats with different levels of resolution and aspect ratios are now competing with one another. CBS and NBC presently broadcast HD at 1920 × 1080; ABC broadcasts at 1280 × 720. Each home HD set has to read the signal it receives and convert it to its own "native" resolution. This conflict will most likely be worked out in time, however, just as it was when stereophonic sound, color television, home video, and almost every other new technology was introduced.

Because so few homes have HD television sets, the networks broadcast only a few programs in HD, but this will increase as the number of home HD sets increases; although home HD sets are still very expensive, the price is dropping steadily. **DVD** (Digital Video Disc) is already having a tremendous impact in the home market, and many homes now have both a VCR (Video Cassette Recorder) and a DVD player. DVD players are already inexpensive, and DVDs themselves, even though they provide much more information, are cheaper to produce than videocassettes ($1 for a DVD, $3 for a VHS tape). Although DVDs are already cheaper to rent, it may be some time before market pressure causes the purchase price of DVDs to fall below those of VHS tapes, but it will happen. Table 13.1 shows the tremendous increase in DVD households and sales projected by the WGA in the coming decade.

In all, more and more films and television shows are being shot in HD every year and the advances in HD technology are coming at a fast pace.

TABLE 13.1   The future of DVD and VHS

	2000	2010
Total U.S. TV households	102 million	113 million
VHS (tape) households	90 million	101 million
DVD (disc) households	13 million	65 million
Total U.S. VHS (tape) sales	$8.15 billion	$6.69 billion
Total U.S. DVD (disc) sales	$2.74 billion	$11.24 billion

George Lucas' *Star Wars: Episode I* contained only three scenes created in video because Lucas did not feel that HD was then sufficiently advanced. Now, just a few years later, he chose to shoot *all* of *Episode 2* in HD, and the time saved allowed the production to finish 5 weeks ahead of schedule. The HD revolution is fully under way.

Summary

Recent advances in high-definition digital video technology have made film-less filmmaking a reality. Early esthetic objections to HD have been answered by recent HD developments; the HD image can now be rendered virtually indistinguishable from film.

Film stock captures an image by a *chemical* process. Light passing through the camera lens falls on the film and activates tiny grains of chemicals contained in the film emulsion. Video, on the other hand, records an image by an *electrical* process. A sensor scans the image coming through the lens and breaks it into dots of light called pixels. These pixels are recorded as digital (on/off) information. Increasing the number of pixels within the video frame increases the level of resolution and produces the high-definition video picture.

Although film is capable of much higher levels of resolution than the HD in common use, the film image degrades every time it is reproduced. As a result, the film image you see in your local theater has about the same resolution as an HD video image.

The illusion of motion in both film and video is created from a sequence of still pictures (frames) that our brain sees as flowing motion. As the number of frames per second is increased, the illusion of motion is enhanced. The movie frame rate of 24 was found to produce a jerky picture in video, so video frame rate was increased to 30 frames per second. Recently video has been developed which produces smooth motion at 24 frames, called 24-frame progressive video, or simply 24p.

Thomas Edison developed a camera with an aspect ratio of 1.33:1, which was the standard for all films until 1953 and remains the standard for ordinary broadcast television. Most feature films today are shot in 1.85:1 or 1.66:1. The most common HD systems use an aspect ratio of 1.78:1, which is also called "16 by 9."

The current HD camera is self-contained and is loaded with a book-size cartridge capable of storing about 40 minutes of material. Shooting is interrupted less to reload the camera and the time saved can be spent doing takes. Best of all, HD dailies are instantaneous. If the final product is delivered in video, there are further savings from the elimination of film negative cutting and color timing is much more flexible in HD than in film.

Digital movies could be transmitted directly to theaters by satellite, eliminating costly prints, if disputes over the high cost of converting theaters to video projection can be resolved. In the meantime, more movies are being shot in HD and transferred to film for distribution.

HD may become the television broadcast standard if the competition between different HD formats can be resolved. DVD (Digital Video Disc) is making a big advance in the home market and a tremendous increase in DVD households and sales is projected in the coming decade. The HD revolution is fully under way.

A Sample Synopsis

The Clyde Charles Story: A Synopsis

By Robert Benedetti

Clyde Charles was a shrimper. He lived quietly in Houma, Louisiana, with his 13 brothers and sisters in a large and devout family with a strong sense of tradition, in the enclave founded by his great-grandfather, the son of slaves. Clyde worked hard and enjoyed a beer with his friends. One night 20 years ago, he was walking home from the local hangout at about 2:30 in the morning when a trooper he knew pulled alongside. The policeman took him to a nearby hospital, to the bedside of a white woman who identified him as the man who had raped her an hour before near the spot where he had been picked up. She had first reported her attacker as bearded, but when clean-shaven Clyde was brought to her bedside, she identified him without hesitation.

At Clyde's trial, his defense team tried to create doubt in the jury's mind by suggesting that his brother, Marlo, who was at the same bar and had walked the same road, had actually committed the crime. But the all-white jury believed the eyewitness identification, and Clyde was given a mandatory life sentence and sent to the notorious Angola prison.

Ten years ago, after 10 years in Angola, Clyde learned about DNA testing. He and his sister began a fight to have the DNA evidence examined. The Terrebone Parish DA fought tooth and nail to withhold the evidence and even tried to destroy it under an old policy. After a prolonged fight to preserve and test the DNA samples, aided by the attention brought to Clyde's case by *CNN Frontline* and Barry Scheck's *Innocence Project*, the test was finally conducted. Clyde was exonerated and released in January of this year.

The authorities ran the DNA identification that had exonerated Clyde through the computers of a national DNA database. By coincidence, Clyde's long-lost brother Marlo was imprisoned in Virginia on a 1992 felony conviction; his DNA was on file, and matched. Marlo was brought back to Louisiana and arrested for the crime.

The sheriff who arrested Clyde has said he thinks the Charles family knew the truth all along, and that Clyde and Marlo switched clothes on the night of the crime in an effort to "beat the system—instead the system beat them." Clyde's lawyers called the sheriff's claim ridiculous. Clyde's sisters believe the sheriff is targeting the family because of the lawsuit Clyde has filed against the prosecutors who denied him access to the DNA evidence for so many years.

Despite the fact that Marlo apparently allowed his brother to languish in jail for 20 years without coming forward, Clyde's sister says that the family will stand by him. "Marlo might be wrong, but be he right or be he wrong, he's still my brother, and I love him. I will hold his hands all the way to the gates of Angola." Clyde himself has said, "I haven't seen or talked to him for 20 years, but when I do I'll hug and kiss him."

The case has been covered by *ABC News, Frontline, Sixty Minutes II,* and many newspaper features. Extensive documentation is available. Robert Benedetti Productions holds the option on Clyde Charles' life story rights.

APPENDIX B

Sample Main Title Credits

Miss Evers' Boys

Card	Main Title Credits
1.	HBO NYC PRESENTS
2.	An ANASAZI PRODUCTION
3.	A JOSEPH SARGENT Film
4.	ALFRE WOODARD
5.	LAURENCE FISHBURNE
6.	CRAIG SHEFFER
7.	MISS EVERS' BOYS
8.	JOE MORTON
9.	OBBA BABATUNDÉ
10.	THOM GOSSOM, JR. VON COULTER
11.	with E. G. MARSHALL as The Senate Chairman
12.	and OSSIE DAVIS as Mr. Evers
13.	Music by CHARLES BERNSTEIN
14.	Choreography by DIANNE McINTYRE
15.	Casting by JAKI BROWN-KARMAN ROBYN M. MITCHELL

16.   Production Designed by
               CHARLES C. BENNETT

17.   Edited by
               MICHAEL BROWN

18.   Director of Photography
               DONALD M. MORGAN, A.S.C.

19.   Producer
               KIP KONWISER

20.   Producer
               DEREK KAVANAGH

21.   Executive Producer
               LAURENCE FISHBURNE

22.   Executive Producer
               ROBERT BENEDETTI

23.   Teleplay by
               WALTER BERNSTEIN

24.   Based on the Play by
               DAVID FELDSHUH

25.   Directed by
               JOSEPH SARGENT

GLOSSARY OF FILM AND TELEVISION TERMS

24p   Progressive 24-frame-per-second digital video, quickly becoming the standard for video production.

A and B rolls   The cut negative ready for printing, with each shot alternating between two rolls so that they marry seamlessly into a single composite print. See also "B roll."

Abby Singer   The next-to-the-last shot of the day.

Above-the-line   The "creative" costs listed in the topmost section of a film budget, such as story and writer costs, actor salaries, director costs, as distinguished from the "technical" costs, which are "below-the-line."

Above-the-title   Credit given to major stars, literally above or before the title of the picture.

Accountant   The person in charge of keeping the extensive books of a film company, issuing the hot cost and weekly cost reports, and handling all payments, salaries, and so on.

Action   What happens in a scene; the script element that describes what happens; what the director calls to start a shot.

AD, First   The director's right-hand person, in charge of all logistics on the set.

AD, Second   The assistant director in charge of personnel, including the placement and timing of all extras in background action. There is also a Second Second, who handles paperwork. All ADs are distinguished by their walkie-talkies.

ADR   Automatic Dialogue Replacement, called "looping," a process whereby dialogue from the production soundtrack is replaced.

Advance   A payment made in advance of rendering service.

AEA   The Actors Equity Association, which has jurisdiction over live theater.

AFTRA   The American Federation of Radio and Television Artists, which has jurisdiction over radio and some forms of television production.

Agent   A talent representative who submits clients for work and makes their deals; must be franchised by the appropriate union. Receives a straight commission of 10% as the only payment for services.

Anamorphic   Wide-screen images are "squeezed" onto a normal 35mm frame by special lenses, then uncompressed when projected.

Angle   The position and view of the camera.

Annotated script   Script with references to source materials for specific elements, used to obtain E & O insurance.

Answer print   The approved print reflecting the final timing.

Arbitration   A process whereby a labor dispute may be settled; how the Writers Guild determines writing credit when a dispute arises.

Art Department Coordinator   Handles the logistics and communications within the art department.

Art Director   The production designer's right-hand person, in charge of rendering the designs for execution.

Aspect Ratio   The proportion of the screen on which the show will be projected. Television is the most narrow, feature films much wider.

Assembly, first   The editor's cut, shown only to the director; also called a rough cut.

Assignment of rights   Passing the rights to a project to someone else, usually to the financing entity.

Attaching talent   Receiving the commitment of an actor, writer, or director to a project as a means of helping to sell the project into development.

Audio time code   The reference numbers on dailies, which are generated from the production sound tapes.

Avid   The most commonly used computer-driven editing system.

B roll   Video shot during production by a visiting crew for use as PR on a show like *Entertainment Tonight*.

Back end   A percentage of the potential profit of the show granted to someone as part of their deal.

Back lot   The standing sets on a studio's grounds, usually including a "New York Street" and other locations.

Background   The elements that complete the environment, including extras, animals, and vehicles.

Base camp   The temporary home of the shooting unit where all the trailers (wardrobe, makeup, honey wagons, grip, electric, etc.) are parked and meals are served. Not to be confused with "home base."

Bell   The signal (on a sound stage) that a take is ready to be made.

Below-the-line   The so-called "technical" costs of the film, as distinguished from the "creative" costs, which are "above-the-line" in a film budget.

Best Boy or Girl   The gaffer's assistant, in charge of electrical equipment.

Big Closeup   The closest shot, face only; also called Extreme Closeup (ECU).

Billing   The placement of credit in the titles.

Blocking   The positions of the actors in sequence throughout the scene, each marked on the floor with colored tape.

Blow up   To enlarge the image in the frame; must be re-photographed as an optical element.

Board   The arrangement of scenes in the order they are to be shot so that they make viable blocks of work.

Boom   A pole on which a microphone is suspended over the heads of the actors.

Breakage   A limited extra payment made by a network when a specific item in the budget costs more than anticipated.

Breakdown   A list of roles to be cast with brief descriptions sent to agents by the casting director. Also, the script broken down by scene to determine the needs of location, talent, and so on, in order to estimate costs.

Budget   The preliminary budget must be approved before a show will be green-lighted; the final budget is issued by the UPM just before shooting starts, after deals are made and other costs are known.

Bundled rights   Copyright covers a number of different rights, such as publication, radio, stage, and so on, which are "bundled" together. The bundle must be untied to isolate certain rights to make deals involving those rights.

Business Affairs Officer   The network or studio executive in charge of the business aspects of a project.

Call   The time of day someone is to report for work.

Callback   A final stage in the casting process when a final selection is made for a role from among a few actors.

Call sheet   The shooting orders for the following day distributed at the end of each day's shooting.

Cameo   A usually brief appearance by a star in a film.

Camera Operator   The head of the camera crew who runs the camera; does the final framing of the shot according to the director's and DP's instructions.

Camera right or left   The direction of the actor movements as seen from the camera.

Card   A typographical display carrying information, such as a credit for one or more persons (single or shared cards), the time and location of the scene, and so on.

Cash-flow deficit   Between scheduled payments from a studio or network, a producer may need to arrange interim or "bridge" financing to carry the costs of the project until the next payment is received.

Casting director   The person who handles all the logistics of the casting process; suggests actors, conducts auditions, and makes the deal when an actor is hired.

Caterer   Supplies the formal meals on location. A movie company, like an army, travels on its stomach.

CGI   Computer Generated Imagery.

Cheating   An adjustment in position, look, or movement by the actor for the sake of the camera's perspective or movement.

Checking the gate   After a scene has been shot, the camera assistant makes sure there was nothing in the mechanism of the camera that could have ruined the film.

Circled takes   The takes identified by the director to be printed.

Clapper board   The board that is photographed at the start of each take to identify the shot and to establish sound synchronization by the "clapping" of a stick or nowadays a digital display.

Click track   When music is supposed to be playing in a scene, the sound mixer may provide the sound of clicking that establishes the tempo so that the actors can dance or react appropriately; this permits the dialogue to be recorded separately from the music for editing.

Close shot A "medium closeup," chest up.

Closeup A tight shot, neck up.

Company All the people working on the show.

Company credit The main title credit for each company that produced or financed a picture.

Company move When the entire unit, with its many trucks, packs up and moves to a new area; almost always done overnight or over the weekend to avoid taking precious shooting time.

Complementary shots Shots that are the same size but from different angles, designed so the editor may cut from one to the other freely.

Completion bond A kind of insurance that helps ensure the completion of the picture by covering cost overruns; costs 4% of the budget and gives some control to the bonding company.

Composite print The print produced when the A and B rolls are combined into a single print.

Construction Coordinator In charge of the carpenters and painters and the shop budgets, responsible for building whatever needs to be built.

Contingency A requirement set by the financing entity, which must be met before production begins, such as the casting of the stars.

Continuity The smooth flow of shots and scenes with no disruptions by incorrect details. The script supervisor has the main responsibility for this during shooting.

Copyright A way of protecting someone's creation from being used without permission; it is established simply by "fixing" the creation in a tangible form that can be verified, such as a publication, a photograph, or a recording.

Cost report Issued weekly, shows how much has been spent for each line of the budget and estimates how much remains to be spent for completion.

Costume Designer In charge of designing, creating, or procuring the clothing worn by the characters.

Cover set An indoor location that is used in place of an outdoor set in case of bad weather.

Coverage The closer shots taken in a scene to be inserted into the master.

Craft services In charge of the omnipresent food and drink on the set; separate from the caterer who serves the formal meals.

Crane A long counterweighted boom that carries the camera and operator aloft and can be moved smoothly. Some cranes have small remote-controlled cameras that can do things a traditional crane cannot.

Creative Executive The network or studio executive who oversees the creative aspects of a project; also called "development executive."

Credits The main creative credits appear in the "main title sequence," the technical credits appear in the "end credits." The very first credits are usually the "company credits" for the financing entities.

Cross   A move by an actor from one position to another.

Cue cards   Cards showing an actor's lines, held on the actor's eye-line.

Cut   (*v*) To edit, to stop the camera. (*n*) A version of the show as edited; the sequence is usually editor's cut, director's cut, producer's cut, and final cut. Also a relatively abrupt change from one shot to another (as distinguished from a more gradual dissolve); there are several kinds of cuts, such as smash cuts and soft cuts. Also, what the director calls to stop a take.

Cutaway   Material inserted in a scene to establish mood, place, or to cover an awkward edit.

D&E   A version of the finished show containing only dialogue and effects, but no music. Used for producing trailers and other promotional material that has its own music.

Day   Whenever the action of the story moves into a new period, it is a new "day." The script days are numbered consecutively no matter how much time elapses between them, as Day One, Day Two, etc.

Day Player   An actor in a smaller role, usually paid by the day, although these parts can sometimes work for weeks.

Deal memo   A short form filled out whenever someone is hired to record the main deal points of salary, schedule, responsibilities, and so on, sometimes used later to prepare a long-form contract.

Deficit   The difference between the licensing fee paid by a network for a movie and the actual cost of production; must be financed by the producer or "deficit financier."

Delivery   The final delivery of the film to the financing entity with all the necessary accompanying material listed in the delivery requirements.

Demographics   The age, gender, and/or economic class of a potential audience.

Depth of field   The narrow range in which the camera's subject is in perfect focus.

Development hell   The period during which the script is written and approved for production.

DGA   The Directors Guild of America.

DGA Trainee   Someone learning to be a director, given certain responsibilities and rights on the set.

Dialogue coach   Really an acting coach; a term left over from the advent of talkies.

Dialogue pre-dub   To ready the dialogue for the final mix to save time on the dubbing stage.

Digital-to-film   Shooting in video then transferring to film for distribution.

Digitize   To render sound or picture into digital form, as when the dailies are fed into the editing machine.

Dissolve   One of the ways of going from one cut to another; a "lap" dissolve overlaps one image with another. Dissolves may be fast, medium, or slow; one may also dissolve (fade) to black or white.

Dolly Grip   The crew member in charge of moving the camera.

DOOD   Day Out of Days: a chart showing when each actor works and correlates the days of shooting with the days of the week and month.

DP   The director of photography, sometimes called a cinematographer; along with the director, responsible for the "look" of the show including lighting and camera placement. In England called "the lighting cameraman."

Double   An actor who replaces another, as in stunt double or photo double; also, when more than one piece of wardrobe is supplied in case the first is ruined.

Downstage   Toward the camera.

Drive-to   A location close enough to the home base that accommodations are not provided by the company.

Dub   From "double," to re-record, as "to dub his voice;" the final mix was once called "the dub" and is done on a "dubbing stage."

DVD   Digital Video Disc. Encodes much more information than a CD.

E & O   Insurance against errors and omissions in the script that may cause lawsuits.

ECU   Extreme closeup (see big closeup).

Editor   The person who assembles or "cuts" the film together to achieve pace, flow, and good storytelling; there are also sound editors, music editors, story editors, and assistant editors.

Effects   Sound effects or visual effects, sometimes written as "FX."

Electrics   Electricians who handle the lighting equipment and cables.

End credits   The "technical" credits.

EPK   The Electronic Press Kit. A video containing interviews and B roll for use by the press.

Equity   See AEA.

Establishing shot   A shot of a location, usually wide, that tells the audience where the action is happening.

Estimator   Someone who specializes in preparing preliminary budgets for scripts.

Eye-line   The placement of the actor's eyes as he or she looks at someone off-camera.

Extras   The people who round out the environment; also called "background."

Fade   When the film image is gradually brought "in" or "out."

Fade to black   The blackout at the end of a scene or film.

Favor   When the camera angle throws more emphasis to one character over another.

Feature film   A film made for theatrical release.

Final cut   Control over the final form of the film, rarely granted by a studio to a director.

Final mix   Combining dialogue, music, and sound effects to produce the final sound track of the film.

First AD   See AD.

First-look deal   When a producer or writer promises a company the first opportunity to produce something he or she develops or writes.

First marks   The opening positions of the actors in a scene.

First team   The principal actors.

Flags   Boards or cloth-covered frames that are used to block the light from a lighting instrument.

Flatbed   A film editing machine on which film is cut manually.

Float   The interest earned by money that is committed but not yet paid out.

Flex file   The Telecine Transfer Log, which carries the various reference numbers (audio and video time codes and film key code) that enable the editor to access specific takes.

Flipping the negative   Reversing the negative in a particular shot, usually to match screen direction in adjoining shots.

Floor manager   In studio television, the director's representative on the floor.

Focus groups   Representative audiences brought in to watch a preview of a film and give their reactions to it.

Focus puller   The first assistant camera person in charge of focus, lenses, filters, etc.

Foley   The creation of sound effects that are synchronized to picture, such as footsteps or glass clinks.

Frame (*n*)   A single still-picture image on the strip of film; also the shape of the picture itself; (*v*) to compose a shot.

Frame rate   The speed at which the frames run; in film, 24, in standard video, 30.

Freeze frame   When a singe frame is frozen by being printed over and over; also refers to the executive producer's credit in some television shows that appears at the end of the story.

Gaffer   The DP's right-hand person, in charge of the lighting crew. The Best Boy or Girl is the gaffer's right-hand person.

Genny   A generator that provides power on location.

Green light   Approval to go into production.

Green screen   A method for photographing an actor in front of a green or blue background, then superimposing his or her image over a different background.

Greens person   The crew person in charge of plants of all kinds.

Grip   A person in charge of moving equipment such as lights or sets. Named after the bag of tools that they used to carry. The head is the Key Grip.

Gross   The total receipts taken in by a picture.

Guarantee   The minimum amount that will be paid; also a letter promising to do something, such as distributing a picture.

Hair stylist   Designs and executes the hair styles for a show.

HD   High definition video.

Hero prop   A prop with special importance often needing special handling by the actor.

High concept   The type of film that is so immediately recognizable that it requires no description, such as "a live-action version of the *X-Men* comics."

Hitting a mark   Taking the proper position.

Holding fee   A fee paid to someone to keep them available for a project.

Home base   The company's center of operations where the production office and communications center is located. Not to be confused with "base camp."

Hook   The quality that sets a project apart and will attract an audience.

Hot cost report   A daily report that highlights any unusual expenditures or savings.

Housekeeping deal   When a studio supports a producer, writer, or actor by providing office space and other infrastructure.

IN   The internegative printed from the interpositive and used for subsequent printing to protect the original negative from the rigors of printing.

In-house production   When a network produces its own films.

Indie   An independently financed film.

Insert   A piece of film shot to be inserted into the master, often a POV or establishing shot.

Insert car   A special truck designed to smoothly carry a camera and lights while towing an action vehicle.

Interlaced video   Standard video in which each frame is scanned twice, once for even-numbered lines, again for odd.

IP   The interpositive printed from the cut negative. Used to make new IN's when needed.

Key   A crew chief; also the principal light source in a scene.

Lap dissolve   See Dissolve.

Layback   To assemble the various elements of the mix into the final product.

Licensing deal   Television networks pay producers a licensing fee for a limited use of a film that covers only part of the production cost.

Line Producer   The producer who handles the details and logistics of the entire company and shoot. Similar to a unit production manager, but with greater creative involvement.

Lined script   The script prepared by the script supervisor with all its notations.

Line-up   When the director, the DP, and the actors go through a scene to establish camera positions.

LLC   A form of financing by a limited liability company.

Local hire   An actor or crew member hired locally when on location.

Location   One of the real places where scenes will be shot.

Location Manager   The person in charge of finding and arranging for locations, as well as arranging parking, directions, route markings, police, traffic, fire protection, etc.

Locking the cut   The point after which no further changes in the visual aspects of the show will be made.

Log line   A brief description of a show used for convenience and for making various lists.

Look   The appearance of the show.

Looping   See ADR and walla.

Long shot   A distant or wide camera position.

LP   A form of financing by a limited partnership.

M&E   A version of the finished show with music and effects only, allowing the insertion of foreign dialogue.

MBA   The minimum business agreement stating the rules and pay scales of a guild or union to which all producers must be signatories.

Made-for-cable   A movie made for broadcast by a cable network such as HBO; usually more costly and more adventurous than a network MOW.

Main title sequence   The opening credits of a film.

Makeup person   In charge of creating and applying makeup.

Manager   Similar to an agent but has greater involvement in the career and even private life of talent; usually receives a 15% commission.

Marks   The position of each actor marked by tape on the floor.

Marquee   The assemblage of supporting players that rounds out the casting appeal of a movie.

Martini   The last shot of the day.

Master   The most inclusive view of a scene, usually shot first.

Match   When one thing can be cut to another without disruption.

Matte   A painted scene that is placed in front of the lens or inserted by composite printing, to replace or extend some of the photographed scene, thereby saving construction costs or creating vistas that would otherwise be impossible.

Mike   Microphone.

Mini-series   A 4- or 6-hour movie broadcast on two or three separate nights.

Mix   See final mix.

Montage   A series of images, usually without dialogue, that forms a single sequence; also the way adjoining images can produce unique meanings.

MOS   Shot silently, "mit out sound."

Movieola   An old-fashioned manual editing machine.

Moving on   Going on to the next scene.

MOW   Movie of the Week, or movie made for television.

Music package   When a composer is paid a lump sum to compose, record, and deliver the music ready to mix.

Negative Cutter   The person who cuts the negative according to the final instructions printed out by the editing machine.

Negative pickup   When a partially or completely finished film is sold for completion or enhancement and eventual distribution.

Net   What is left after all costs have been deducted from the gross receipts. A very rare commodity.

New deal   Moving on to the next scene.

Notes   Comments on a script, performance, dailies, etc., requesting changes.

Offering/prospectus   The document given to prospective investors in a film describing the project and its potential.

On a bell   When the set is "locked down" during shooting on a television soundstage.

On hold   When an actor is actually scheduled to work, but must be quickly available in case they are needed.

On location   Working away from the sound stage or away from the home city.

One-liner   A short version of the shooting schedule.

Optical   When film must be re-photographed to superimpose material, create a dissolve, blow up the image, or for some other reason, it is sent to an optical house. The re-photographed film is then inserted into the final negative.

Optical sound track   The results of the final mix are transferred to a visual form and printed in the margin of a release print.

Option   A fee paid to control a property for a specific period in hopes that it can eventually be purchased.

Orchestra Contractor   The person who hires the musicians.

Over-cranking   Shooting in slow motion by speeding up the camera.

P&A   Prints and Ads; the money committed up front by a distribution company to market and distribute a film.

PA   Production assistant. These people usually wear walkie-talkies and do whatever needs doing on the set.

Packaging   Some agencies will provide a number of their clients for a project as a package, for which the agency receives a substantial fee; generally resisted by networks and studios.

Pages   A short written description of a project used in the pitching process.

Partner Someone who has invested in a film and shares in both the risk and the chance for profit; in an LP, the limited partners have a limited risk and reward, the general partner has unlimited risk and reward.

Pay or play A deal in which the person will be paid whether they perform services or not.

Perks Perquisites granted to certain people, such as special accommodations, support personnel, and so on.

PGA The Producers Guild of America.

Pickup A portion of a scene to be reshot.

Pitch Presenting a project to a potential buyer.

Pixel A tiny dot of color that with many others comprises the video picture.

Plagiarism Stealing from someone else's work.

Playback When a scene requires music, the sound mixer plays it during shooting to allow for lip or movement synchronization. If the dialogue needs to be recorded separately from the music, a click track may be used instead.

Points The percentage points of profit participation granted to some artists.

Polish The final step in a writing deal; a pass at a completed script to make slight improvements.

Post The period after the shoot when the film is edited and completed.

Post-production Supervisor The person who guides the film through the post-production process; in television called the associate or co-producer.

POV A shot from someone's point of view.

Prelay Sound material prepared in advance for the final mix.

Prep The period before the shoot when preparations are made.

Presale The advance sale of some specific right to a project, such as the foreign distribution rights, to raise funds for production.

Preview A private showing of a film at an early stage of completion to obtain feedback of a sample audience.

Print One version of the edited film; there are trial prints leading to an answer print.

Print it What the director tells the script supervisor when he or she wants a shot to appear on the dailies; may also signal that work on a shot is done, although not always.

Process Shooting to create an effect, such as being in traffic or flying, often using rear projection. "Poor man's process" is the same using lighting or other effects instead of rear projection.

Process trailer A low trailer used to carry an action vehicle, camera, and lights for shooting driving scenes.

Producer The person who guides a film through all phases of its creation. There are various kinds of producing credits, such as executive producer, line producer, associate producer, and co-producer.

Producer's Rep Someone who specializes in selling independent films, often a lawyer.

Production Accountant   The person in charge of recording and reporting all financial activity of the film company.

Production bonus   A bonus paid to a writer if his or her script is actually produced.

Production Coordinator   The person in charge of all communication within the film company and with the outside world.

Production Designer   The artist responsible for creating the visual world of the film by designing sets, supervising dressing, coordinating the costumes, etc.

Production Executive   The network or studio executive who is in charge of the actual production of a film.

Production meeting   The final event of prep, when all department heads gather to go through the script together.

Production report   The daily report on the unit's work showing how many setups were done, which scenes were completed, how much film was used, etc.

Production track   The sound recorded when the show was shot.

Prop Master   Person in charge of everything handled by the actors.

Prosthetic   A molded rubber piece applied to an actor to alter his or her appearance.

Public domain   When published material is so old that it is no longer protected by copyright.

Pulldown   Technique for transferring 30-frame video to 24-frame film.

Quote   The recent fee and credit earned by an artist on which a new offer is based.

Rack focus   To change focus from one subject to another during a shot.

Radio mike   A microphone hidden in the actor's clothes that broadcasts to a receiver nearby.

Rainbow script   The shooting script with all its changed colored pages in place.

Reading offer   An offer to a star or director in which they read the script before agreeing to participate in the project.

Reccie   Reconnaissance; see technical scout.

Registration   Registering a script or treatment with the copyright office or depositing it with the Writers Guild to prove authorship and date of composition.

Release prints   The prints sent to theaters.

Re-shoot   To redo a portion of a film after wrap.

Research report   An examination of the script to check facts and to clear the use of proper names.

Resolution   The degree of sharpness of an image.

Rigging crew   A crew that comes to the set ahead of time (even overnight) to prepare for shooting.

Rights   The right to control something; there are life-story rights, book and play rights, music rights (which include both master rights and publishing rights), and so on.

Roll it   The call from the First AD to start the sound recorder, answered by the call of "speed" when the production sound mixer is recording.

Rolling   When the sound recorder is running, everyone on the set must be absolutely quiet.

Rough cut   The first assembly of a scene or film. See also Cut.

Run   One showing of a film.

Runaway production   Most film production is now in Canada and other countries where costs are lower.

SAG   The Screen Actors Guild; the union with jurisdiction over film actors.

Schedule   The days of shooting.

Schedule of payments   The schedule on which payments will be made; see Cash-flow deficit.

Scoring session   The recording of the film's music.

Screening auditions   The preliminary auditions conducted by the casting director from which callbacks are made.

Scrims   Panels of screening that diffuse or reduce the light from an instrument.

Script Supervisor   The person in charge of continuity; must remember every detail of every shot. They also prepare a lined script that shows what the duration and nature of each shot was; this is invaluable to the editor. An unsung hero.

Second AD   See AD.

Second camera   To save time, two cameras will sometimes cover a scene simultaneously.

Second Team   The stand-ins who substitute for the first team while the lighting is done.

Second Unit   A small unit that works separately from the main company to shoot certain material.

Set   Where a scene is being shot, whether it is a real place or was built.

Set Decorator   Person in charge of the items that dress the set.

Setup   A camera position and all the attendant lighting, laying of track, etc.

Shoot   The period of actual filming.

Shooting ratio   The amount of film a director uses to produce a usable result.

Shooting schedule   A detailed list of sequence of the scenes to be shot and everything needed for each.

Shooting script   The script as prepared for shooting, marked with the scenes and major shots.

Shot   One piece of film.

Shot list   In three-camera television, the sequence of shots each camera must get during a scene; in single-camera film, a list of the day's work that the director may prepare.

Shot size   The framing, as in closeup, medium shot, long shot, etc.

Showrunners   The writer-producers in charge of a television series or sitcom.

Sides   The half-size pages of script distributed each day, containing the scenes to be shot that day.

Single   A shot containing only one actor.

Slate   To identify a shot; this is done for the camera by the clapper board and verbally by the sound mixer on the production tape.

Slo-mo   Slow motion, either created by speeding up the camera or double-printing frames of the film.

Smash cut   A jarring, abrupt cut.

Soft cut   Actually a four- or six-frame dissolve.

Sound mixer   The production sound mixer on the set; there are also sound mixers who do the re-recording of the show with sound effects and music in the final mix.

Sound stage   A building especially prepared for filming.

Sound track   The sound of the film, usually printed on the edge of the film and read optically, hence an "optical sound track."

Sounds like   Music written by the composer to imitate source music, thereby avoiding the need to purchase music rights for authentic material.

Source music   Music coming from a radio, jukebox, band, or other "live" source within a scene.

Speed   See Roll it.

Splinter unit   A very small unit that goes off to get a particular shot; also called a second camera unit.

Spotting   Locating where the sound effects and music will go in the locked cut.

Stage   A sound stage, a special building designed for film production.

Stage Right or Left   Movement from the actor's perspective as they face the camera.

Stand-in   A double for an actor who takes the actor's place during lighting.

Step deal   An agreement involving several stages.

Still Photographer   Takes PR pictures during shooting using a soundproof camera.

Stock footage   Footage available from a "stock house," which may be purchased for use instead of shooting from scratch; often used for establishing shots of famous locations.

Storyboard   A series of drawings showing the composition of each shot in a sequence or film.

Strip   A single column containing the specifics of each scene, placed in a board and used for planning purposes..

Stunt coordinator   Person in charge of all fights, falls, crashes, or other stunts, and especially safety in their execution.

Subtext   The feelings and thoughts of a character expressed without dialogue by the actor; of tremendous interest and importance for the camera, which "photographs thought."

Supervising Sound Editor   The person who guides the film through the audio portion of post-production.

Swing gang   The crew that prepares the set for shooting.

Synopsis   A brief condensation of a story used for pitching.

Table reading   An early rehearsal at which the cast reads the script aloud.

Take   A version of a shot.

Taping   The final performance of a sitcom, usually with a live audience.

Technical Director   In television, the person who actually switches from camera to camera at the director's instruction.

Technical scout   Near the end of Prep, the director takes key people to each location and describes the shooting to be done at each.

Telecine   The machine or process that transfers film to videotape.

Teleprompter   A monitor that shows an actor's lines; see Cue cards.

Temp music and effects   Music and effects inserted by the editor in an early version of the film to give an impression of what is intended for the final product.

Time code   The reference numbers used to locate and synchronize frames.

Timing   Adjusting the color, brightness, and other aspects of the picture through adjustments in the printing process; the same decisions must be made when transferring the film to video. These processes are done by "timers." Also the estimate of the length of each scene made before shooting starts, and the record of the length of each scene as actually shot.

Timer   The technician who makes adjustments in the film printing process to achieve the desired look in each shot; the same function is served by a video timer when transferring to video.

Top sheet   The summary page of a film budget.

Track   Moving the camera to follow the action, often on an actual track.

Transfer   To translate from film to video, or vice versa.

Transportation Coordinator   In charge of all vehicles and company moves; the transportation captain is in charge of the drivers.

Treatment   The first written form of a show outlining the scenes, major characters, action, and locations; usually the first step in a writer's deal; called the "story" in television.

Turnaround   The time off that must be guaranteed to an actor or crew member between work days; different in various situations. Also the granting of the right to a producer or writer to attempt to sell an abandoned project elsewhere.

Two-shot   A shot containing two actors.

Underscore   The music for the film.

UPM   Unit production manager; see line producer.

Upstage   Away from the camera.

Video assist   A video feed coming directly from the camera lens that can be viewed on a monitor during shooting.

Video time code   The reference numbers generated in dailies when they are transferred to videotape.

WGA   The Writers Guild of America.

Walla   Adding the human sounds, such as crowd noises and telephone voices, which complete the environment. This is the business of "loop groups."

Wardrobe   What costumes are called in film.

Wardrobe Supervisor   The costume designer's right-hand person, responsible for the execution and maintenance of the costumes.

Whiteout   Fading to white.

Wild lines   Lines of dialogue recorded without picture for possible use by the editor.

Windows   The small displays of time or key codes on dailies.

Wiping   A cut from shot to shot that moves across the frame; also when an extra or vehicle passes in front of the lens during a scene.

Works   The wardrobe, hair, and makeup process, as "he's in the works."

Wrap   The end of work, be it a day, the entire picture, or this book.

INDEX

NOTE

This index does not duplicate the items listed in the Table of Contents. It also does not list the many film titles that appear in the text, although it does reference all persons mentioned, and the ongoing examples taken from *Miss Evers' Boys*. Common phrases such as "camera angle" and "shooting schedule" are alphabetized according to the first word of the phrase.